S L O V E N E

Dictionary & Phrasebook

HIPPOCRENE DICTIONARY & PHRASEBOOKS

Albanian	Latvian
Arabic (Eastern Arabic)	Lithuanian
Arabic (Modern Standard)	Malagasy
Armenian (Eastern)	Maltese
Armenian (Western)	Mongolian
Australian	Nepali *Romanized*
Azerbaijani	Norwegian
Basque	Pashto *Romanized*
Bosnian	Pilipino (Tagalog)
Breton	Polish
British	Portuguese (Brazilian)
Cajun French	Punjabi
Chechen	Québécois
Croatian	Romanian
Czech	Romansch
Danish	Russian
Dari *Romanized*	Serbian
Esperanto	Shona
Estonian	Sicilian
Finnish	Slovak
French	Slovene
Georgian	Somali
German	Spanish (Latin American)
Greek	Swahili
Hebrew *Romanized*	Swedish
Hindi	Tajik
Hungarian	Tamil *Romanized*
Igbo	Thai *Romanized*
Ilocano	Turkish
Irish	Ukrainan
Italian	Urdu *Romanized*
Japanese *Romanized*	Uzbek
Korean	Vietnamese
Lao *Romanized*	

SLOVENE
Dictionary & Phrasebook

NINA SNOJ

SLOVENE-ENGLISH
ENGLISH-SLOVENE

HIPPOCRENE BOOKS, INC.
New York

ISBN 0-7818-1047-7

Publisher: George Blagowidow
Editors: Robert Stanley Martin, Nicholas Williams
Slovene copyeditor: Marta Steinberger
Book design and composition: Susan A. Ahlquist
Cover design: Ronnie McBride
Cover photo: Tolmin and the Soča bridge from the air, by Matevž
    Lenarčič; property of LTO Sotočje. Used with permission.

For information, address:
    Hippocrene Books, Inc.
    171 Madison Avenue
    New York, NY 10016
    www.hippocrenebooks.com

Cataloging-in-Publication data available from the Library of Congress.

Printed in the United States of America.

Table of Contents

Abbreviations

adj.	Adjective
adv.	Adverb
conj.	Conjunction
du.	Dual
f.	Feminine
interj.	Interjection
m.	Masculine
n.	Noun
nt.	Neuter
num.	Numeral
pl.	Plural
prep.	Preposition
pron.	Pronoun
sing.	Singular
v.	Verb
admin.	Administration
autom.	Automobile
bot.	Botanics
bus.	Business
cin.	Cinema
cloth.	Clothing
col.	Color
coll.	Colloquial
comm.	Commerce
comp.	Computer
constr.	Construction
culin.	Culinary
cust.	Customs
fam.	Familiar
form.	Formal
gram.	Grammar

insult	Insult
law	Law
lit.	Literature
mar.	Maritime
milt.	Military
relig.	Religion
sp.	Sport
tec.	Technical
tel.	Telephone
theat.	Theatre
trans.	Transport
univ.	University
vulg.	Vulgar
zool.	Zoology

Instructions

In Slovene, the gender is definitive when it comes to endings; the verb and the adjective are strongly influenced by it. In dictionaries the most commonly used gender is masculine, from which you can easily derive a feminine version if you use the following rules. For most adjectives, you simply add -*a*, and for nouns you have a couple of main choices: (-ka, -ica).

1. **lep** *adj.* beautiful   lep**a**
2. **star** *adj.* old   star**a**
3. **prijazen** *adj.* kind   prijazn**a**

4. **govoriti** *v.* to talk   govoril je *(m.)*, govoril**a** je *(f.)*
5. **hoditi** *v.* to walk   hodil je *(m.)*, hodil**a** je *(f.)*
6. **biti** *v.* to be   on je *(m.)*, on**a** je *(f.)*

7. **Japonec** *n.m.* Japanese   Japon**ka**
8. **pevec** *n.m.* singer   pev**ka**
9. **športnik** *n.m.* athlete   športni**ca**
10. **učitelj** *n.m.* professor   učitelj**ica**
11. **vegetarijanec** *n.m.* vegetarian   vegetarijan**ka**

In the phrasebook, the difference is indicated as follows:

I would like to watch the TV.
Rad(a) bi gledal(a) televizijo.

Rad bi gledal televizijo. *(m.)*
Rad**a** bi gledal**a** televizijo. *(f.)*

Introduction to the
Slovene Language

This phrasebook will help you communicate wherever Slovene is spoken. This includes Slovenia, Austrian Carintha, and the neighboring Italian provinces of Trieste, Gorizia, and Udine. Knowledge of at least a few Slovene words and phrases is of great use in everyday situations, such as shopping, ordering food, and looking for accommodations. The best source of information when traveling in Slovene-speaking areas is, without a doubt, the local population, and knowledge of the language is an incomparable aid to finding things out. An added benefit is the rapport one develops with the people by demonstrating interest in their language. It is difficult to understand the complexity of a language without knowing anything of its history, and this is doubly so of Slovene, given its native region's unstable past. Given that, you may enjoy learning more about the history of the Slovene language.

Language Group and Similar Languages

Slovene is an Indo-European language that, along with Serbo-Croatian, comprises the western group of southern Slavic languages. Given the geographical proximity between the languages' native regions, the similarity between the two would seem obvious, although it appears easier for Slovenes to understand Serbo-Croatian than the other way around. This may be due to the fact that, in the old Yugoslavia, Serbo-Croatian was the most widely spoken language in the country, and short courses in it were taught in all Slovene elementary schools. As a result, most Slovenes are bilingual and there is a marked cultural ability to easily learn other languages. (Most Slovenes also speak either English, German, Italian, or Hungarian.) As for the Slovene language, it has a number of features characteristic of the majority of Slavic languages in the areas of phonology, morphology, and lexicology. It also shares a highly developed inflectional system, which includes the preservation of the dual and genitive case in inflectional form. (See the Grammar section.)

Speaking of Territory and Numbers

Slovene is the official language of the Republic of Slovenia and Slovene minorities in Austria, Italy and Hungary. It is also spoken by Slovenian immigrant groups in the United States (particularly Ohio), Canada, Argentina, and Australia. The Slovene-speaking area of Europe (bordered by Austria in the north, Hungary and Croatia to the east and south, and Italy to the west) reaches further west than any other Slavic group. It once extended as far as Venice, Italy.

Slovene is the mother tongue of 90 percent of the country's 2 million people, and there are another half-million speakers around the world. It is characterized by a great number of dialects, which indicates its great age. Language experts have established the presence of 46 distinct dialects, which divide into seven regional groups: Carinthian, Upper Carniolan, Lower Carniolan, Littoral, Rovte, Styrian and Pannonian. There is, however, a general sense of contemporary Slovene among Slovenians that will allow you to get by wherever the language is spoken.

Education and Grammar

The dialect used in this book is known as Contemporary Standard Slovene. It is the language presented in grammars and taught in schools and universities. As such, it is the language of educated Slovenes and used in the media and the arts. One must remember that the Slovene people are exceptionally proud of their language. Despite many efforts to wipe it out, the language gave them a sense of national identity unity over centuries of repression by outside rulers.

Contemporary Slovene is grammatically complex, with three genders, four verb tenses, and six cases for nouns, pronouns, and adjectives. In addition to the singular and plural cases, Slovene has something rare in linguistics: the dual number case. Not only is there *cesta* (street) and *ceste* (streets), but also *dve cesti* (two streets). Things become even more complicated when one considers the special endings indicating gender, number, and the different classes of nouns.

Slovenian uses the Roman alphabet. There are 25 letters, and three have diacritical marks (or, in Slovenian, *strešica,* which means "little roof"). The three letters are č, š, ž and they are pronounced "ch," "sh," and "je". As in English, there are different values for vowels. For instance, the vowels *o* and *e* may be stressed or unstressed, long or short, open or closed, and so on.

The number of verbs is much smaller than that in Germanic and Romance languages. Verbs have been simplified and now have only one past tense, one present tense, and one future tense. The archaic supine (a verb form used in a way similar to the infinitive) has been preserved along with the infinitive. As in other Slavic languages, the aspect category of verbs (an indication of the nature of a verb's activity) has been expanded.

The Slovene government requires that all children receive eight years of primary education and four years of secondary education. Although not required by law, most students receive post-secondary levels of education or higher. There are 30 institutions of higher education in Slovenia, and among them is the University of Ljubljana, which was founded in 1919.

Slovene Language and Culture Today

The contemporary Slovene language is a fully developed and richly structured modern language. It is gaining significant interest as a foreign language (taught in Slovenia as well as in other universities abroad) and works exceptionally well in the translated version of the Windows 2000 operating system. Given the proximity of neighboring cultures, such as Italian in the west and German in the north, and the fact that all foreign movies are shown with subtitles, there are a lot of "borrowed" words in the Slovenian vocabulary. Some come from the English language (*marketing*, *video*, *skateboard*, *fine*), others from German (*cajt – Zeit*, meaning time) and yet others from Italian and French (*atelje – ateile*, meaning workshop, and *miza – mesa*, meaning table). An abundance of cultural events keep the language alive. These include folk festivals, street theater, and live concerts. There are also the marathon readings in public squares every February 8, the country's cultural day and the day of remembrance for Slovenia's national poet, France Prešern.

Slovenia is now a parliamentary republic. The Parliament is composed of the State Council and the Chamber of Deputies, where a seat is saved for the officially recognized Italian and Hungarian minorities. The President of the Republic is elected every five years.

The lifestyle of Slovenes, in which they enjoy the benefits of modern technology and, at the same time, live a stress-free life in a clean and peaceful environment, is still a surprise to many foreign visitors. Slovenes love to travel, but they also love their home, and the immigration rate from this country is practically nil. The current situation in Slovenia seems to contain some sort of general optimism regarding the European Union, but at the same time, some skeletons have been left in the closet, ones that should have been cleaned out a long time ago. There is a certain irony in the fact that the nation, which has spent the greater part of its history fighting for independence, voted to integrate into yet another union of countries. While the public and the politicians are busy dealing with yet another transition, the general opinion about the past Yugoslav experience is divided, as someone once said, between a feeling described as "yugonostalgia" and historical amnesia.

Slovene Grammar

Nouns – Genders – Grammatical Number –
Cases – Verb Tenses and Aspects of Verbs –
Adjectives – Pronouns – Adverbs – Numerals –
Conjunctions – Prepositions

Nouns
Samostalniki

Nouns in Slovene, as in English, are words that
denote people and things. Slovenian nouns **change
their endings** when you use them in the dual or
plural, and these depend on their context within a
sentence (see Cases).

To je sosedova **hiša**.
*This is the neighbor's
    house.*

Ne najdem tvoje **hiše**.
*I can't find your
    house.*

V rumeni **hiši** na
    koncu ulice.
*In the yellow house at
    the end of the street.*

Avto je parkiran
    za **hišo**.
*The car is parked
    behind the house.*

Genders
Spol

Slovene nouns can be grouped according to gender,
which is either masculine, feminine, or neutral. Pay
attention to the following rules, although be aware
that there are many exceptions to them.

Masculine nouns end in a consonant, or, rather, have no ending:

bull	plate	glass	step	horse
bik	**krožnik**	**kozarec**	**korak**	**konj**

Feminine nouns generally end in *–a* or *–i*:

flower	house	painting	table
roža	**hiša**	**slika**	**miza**

Neutral nouns end in *–o* and *–e*:

city	beer	letter	egg
mesto	**pivo**	**pismo**	**jajce**

Grammatical Number
Slovnično Število

In addition to the plural and singular, Slovene has separate forms for the dual (as in *both*).

Gender	Singular (1)	Dual (2)	Plural (3 or more)
Feminine	Omara *(closet)*	Omar**i**	Omar**e**
Masculine	Telefon *(telephone)*	Telefon**a**	Telefon**i**
Neuter	Mesto *(city)*	Mest**i**	Mest**a**

Appreciate the difference between the following sentences:

Dual: **Greva** plesat?
Shall we dance?

Plural: **Gremo** plesat?
Shall we dance?

Case
Sklon

Slovene nouns, adjectives, and pronouns take cases. Their endings change, and how they change is determined by the relationship between the words in a sentence. There are six cases in Slovene. The nominative case defines the subject of a sentence. All other cases define either a direct or an indirect object.

Case	Feminine (sing.)	Masculine (sing.)	Neuter (sing.)
Nominative	punc**a** (girl)	fant (boy)	mest**o** (city)
Genitive	punc**e**	fant**a**	mest**a**
Dative	punc**i**	fant**u**	mest**u**
Accusative	punc**o**	fant**a**	mest**o**
Locative	(pri) punc**i**	(pri) fant**u**	(pri) mest**u**
Instrumental	(s) punc**o**	(z) fant**om**	(z) mest**om**

The locative and instrumental can only be formed with prepositions.

Jutri (tomorrow) se dobimo **pri mostu**.
We shall meet tomorrow at the bridge.

Z Ano sva v parku.
I am in the park with Ana.

Verb Tenses and Verb Aspects
Glagolski Čas in Glagolski Vid

Verb Aspects
Glagolski Vid

Slovene verbs distinguish between the perfective and imperfective aspects, which means they differ between completed actions and incomplete ones. Basic or simple verbs are generally imperfective and normally don't carry a prefix or suffix:

skakati (imperfective verb)
to jump (continuously)

skočiti (perfective verb)
to jump (once)

Prefixing creates additional, usually perfective, meanings:

preskočiti   preskakovati
to jump over (once)   *to be jumping over continuously*

Verb Tenses
Glagolski Čas

Standard Slovene verb tenses have been reduced to four: the present, past perfect, past simple, and future, although the past perfect tense is almost never used.

Present *(to think)*

	Singular	Plural	Dual
1st pers	mislim	mislimo	misliva
2nd pers	misliš	mislite	mislita
3rd pers	misli	mislijo	mislita

Auxiliaries–Past tense *(to be)*

	Singular	Plural	Dual
1st pers	sem	smo	sva
2nd pers	si	ste	sta
3rd pers	je	so	sta

Auxiliaries–Future tense *(to be)*

	Singular	Plural	Dual
1st pers	bom	bomo	bova
2nd pers	boš	boste	bosta
3rd pers	bo	bodo	bosta

Form sentences according to the following rule:

To be + participle ending in –l (*m.*) or –la (*f.*)

Bral **sem** knjigo.
I was reading a book.

Bom premislil.
I will think it through.

Hodil **sem** dva dni.
I walked for two days.

Si kupil kruh?(*sing.*)
Did you buy bread?

Bosta vstopila?
Will you (two) come in?

Bili **smo** v Alpah.

We were in the Alps.

Bomo uspeli priti pravočasno?
Will we be able to get there on time?

Negation

Sentence negation requires the use of negative prefixes :

Bil sem v mestu.
I was downtown.

Nisem bil v mestu.
I wasn't downtown.

Stanovanje **je** veliko. Stanovanje **ni** veliko.
The apartment is big. The apartment isn't big.

In Slovene, double negation is a correct form, although it sometimes causes confusion as to whether the affirmative or the negative is meant by a given sentence. For example:

Ne poznam nikogar.
I don't know anyone (lit. *I don't know nobody*)

Adjectives
Pridevniki

Adjectives express three main ideas: **quality** (qualitative adjectives), **relation** (relational adjectives) and **possession** (possessive adjectives).

Slovene is an inflectional language. Nouns, pronouns and adjectives agree in **case**, **number**, and **gender**. Adjectives also change their endings, and, in most of the cases, they share the ending of the noun.

kind
prijazen

prijazn**a** gospa   prijazen**ø** učitelj**ø**   prijazn**o** mest**o**
kind lady   *kind teacher*   *kind city*

Comparative and Superlative
Primerjalnik in presežnik

Comparison denotes degrees of intensity in adjectives and some adverbs. A prefix and suffix are often used, although there are many exceptions to this rule. There are two degrees that express gradation:

good   better   the best
dober   **boljši**   **najboljši**

	Comparative	Superlative
big	bigger	the biggest
velik	**večji**	**največji**
bad	worse	the worst
slab	**slabši**	**najslabši**
fast	faster	the fastest
hiter	**hitrejši**	**najhitrejši**
green	greener	the greenest
zelen	**bolj zelen**	**najbolj zelen**

Moj avto je **najhitrejši**.
My car is the fastest.

Trava je vedno **bolj zelena** na sosedovi strani.
The grass is always greener on the other side.

Jana je **večja** kot Katja.
Jana is bigger then Katja.

Pronouns
Zaimki

Personal pronouns (osebni zaimek) all take cases.

Singular	Dual, masc. (2)	Plural (3 or more), masc.
Jaz sem	**Midva** sva	**Mi** smo
I am	*We are*	*We are*
Ti si	**Vidva** sta	**Vi** ste*
You are	*You two are*	*You are*

*Also used when addressing somebody respect-fully or in formal situations.

On/ona je **Onadva** sta   **Oni** so
He/she is   *They are*   *They are*

Possessive pronouns (svojilni zaimek)

Singular	Dual (2)	Plural (3 or more)
Moj-a *Mine*	**Najin-a** *Ours (2)*	**Naš-a** *Ours*
Tvoj-a *Yours*	**Vajin-a** *Yours (2)*	**Vaš-a*** *Yours*
Njegov-a *His*	**Njun-a** *Theirs (2)*	**Njihov-a** *Theirs*
Njen-a je *Her*		

*Also used when addressing somebody respect-fully or in formal situations.

Reflexive personal pronouns (povratni osebni zaimek)

The reflexive pronoun in Slovene is *se* or *sebe*. It is the same for all persons and grammatical numbers; that it, it is dependent solely on case. *Se* (*sebe*) is the accusative form of the reflexive pronoun.

Dative   Umivam *si* roke.
                I am washing my hands.

Accusative   Umivam *se.*
                I am washing myself.

Pronouns are usually dropped unless the person is emphasized or the reference is changed during the discourse.

Instead of:

Jaz govorim angleški in španski jezik.
I speak English and Spanish.

you can say

Govorim angleški in španski jezik.
I speak English and Spanish.

Adverbs
Prislovi

Adverbs are generally formed from adjectives by adding the suffixes –o or –ma:

Kosilo je bilo **dobro**.
The lunch was delicious.

Bilo je **lepo**.
It was nice.

There are four main types of adverb: adverbs of time *(today)*, adverbs of place *(home)*, adverbs of manner *(completely)*, and adverbs of cause and reason *(on purpose)*.

dobro	slabo
well	*badly*
malo	veliko
a little	*a lot*
dovolj	nekaj
enough	*some*

mrzlo	toplo	vroče
cold	*warm*	*hot*

včeraj	danes	jutri
yesterday	*today*	*tomorrow*

zjutraj	zvečer
in the morning	*in the evening*

dopoldne	popoldne
in the morning	*in the afternoon*

ponoči	podnevi
at night	*day time*

poleti	jeseni
in summer	*in autumn*

pozimi	spomladi
in winter	*in spring*

zmeraj	nikoli
always	*never*

tukaj	tam
here	*there*

zunaj	notri
outside	*inside*

spredaj	zadaj
in front	*at the back*

Numerals
Števniki

Numerals in Slovene are, grammatically speaking, similar to adjectives. They take cases in agreement with the nouns they are related to.

Cardinal Numerals

1	ena
2	dve
3	tri
4	štiri
5	pet
6	šest
7	sedem
8	osem
9	devet
10	deset
11	enajst
12	dvanajst
13	trinajst
14	štirinajst
15	petnajst
16	šestnajst
17	sedemnajst
18	osemnajst
19	devetnajst
20	dvajset
21	enaindvajset
22	dvaindvajset
23	triindvajset
24	štiriindvajset
25	petindvajset
26	šestindvajset

27	sedemindvajset
28	osemindvajset
29	devetindvajset
30	trideset
40	štirideset
50	petdeset
60	šestdeset
70	sedemdeset
80	osemdeset
90	devetdeset
100	sto
82	dvainosemdeset
390	tristo devetdeset
8, 200	osem tisoč dvesto
1,000,000	en milijon

Kupil sem šest knjig.
I bought six books.

Stara je šestintrideset let.
She is thirty-six years old.

Ordinal Numbers

1st	prvi
2nd	drugi
3rd	tretji
4th	četrti
5th	peti
6th	šesti
7th	sedmi
8th	osmi
9th	deveti
10th	deseti

30th	trideseti
125th	stopetindvajseti

Danes je drugi dan tekmovanja.
Today is the second day of the competition.

Dobrodošli na dvainštiridesetem letnem srečanju!
Welcome to the forty-second annual meeting!

Conjunctions
Vezniki

Conjunctions connect words in a sentence. Most conjunctions in Slovene require a comma in front of them and significantly affect the word order.

in	Kupil sem kruh **in** mleko.
and	*I bought bread and milk.*
ker	Pozen sem, **ker** sem zamudil avtobus.
because	*I am late because I missed the bus.*
da	Prosil me je, **da** mu pomagam.
for, to	*He asked me to help him.*
ampak,toda	Klical sem te, **ampak** ni te bilo doma.
but	*I called you, but you weren't home.*
čeprav	Ne strinjam se, ***čeprav*** imaš na nek način prav.
although	*I disagree, although you are right in a way.*
ko, kadar	Piši mi, **ko** boš imela čas.
when	*Write me when you can.*

| ki | To je igralka, **ki** je dobila nagrado. |
| *that* | *This is the actress who has won the award.* |

| kateri | **Kateri** avto si kupila? |
| *which* | *Which car did you buy?* |

| če | **Če** hočeš, lahko pridem pote. |
| *If* | *If you want, I can pick you up.* |

Prepositions
Predlogi

Each preposition requires a specific case, and Slovene prepositions don't always match literal English translations.

| iz, s/z | Prihajam **iz** Pariza. |
| *from* | *I am coming from Paris.* |

| brez | Hočem eno kavo **brez** sladkorja. |
| *without* | *I want one sugarless coffee.* |

| od | Tukaj živimo **od** leta 1996. |
| *from, since* | *We have been living here since 1996.* |

| do | **Do** kdaj boš odsoten? |
| *until* | *Until when will you be away?* |

| zraven | Sedi **zraven** mene. |
| *beside* | *Sit beside me.* |

| blizu | Šola je **blizu** avtobusne postaje. |
| *close* | *The school is close to the bus stop.* |

| k/h | Pridemo **k** tebi? |
| *at, to* | *Shall we come to your place?* |

proti	Vozim se **proti** letališču.
towards	*I am driving towards the airport.*
čez	**Čez** cesto živi moja najboljša prijateljica.
across	*My best friend lives across the street.*
v	Gremo **v** kino.
in, to, into	*Let's go to the cinema.*
na	Kosilo je **na** mizi.
on	*Lunch is on the table.*
ob	Sprehajal sem se **ob** reki.
by	*I took a walk by the river.*
za	Skril se je **za** drevo.
behind	*He hid behind the tree.*
pod	**Pod** nami stanuje moja teta.
below	*My aunt lives below us.*
med	Rojstni dan sem praznoval **med** prijatelji.
between	*I celebrated my birthday with my friends.*
o	Gledali smo film **o** medvedih.
about	*We were watching a movie about bears.*
pri	Počakaj me **pri** vhodu.
at	*Wait for me at the entrance.*
s/z	**Z** njimi je lahko shajati.
with, from	*It is easy to get along with them.*

Pronunciation Guide

The Slovene alphabet (*abeceda*) is a modification of the Roman alphabet as adapted from Czech by Ljudevit Gaj in the nineteenth century. The Slovene alphabet has 25 letters. It does not have the letters *w*, *q*, *x*, and *y*. They are represented as a composition of Slovenian letters (*q* is *ku*, *x* is *iks*, and so on.), but you have to learn three new letters: č (pronounced like *ch* in *ch*air), š (like *sh*, as in *sh*eep), and ž (like *zh*, as in mea*s*ure). As in English, there are different values for vowels. For example, the vowels *o* and *e* may be stressed or unstressed, long or short, open or closed.

Special Pronunciation Rules that Apply in the Slovene Language

- **D** and **Ž** together are pronounced like the English *j*:

  Mad̲ž̲arska Hungary (as in **J**ane)

- **L** and **V** at the end of a word or before another consonant are pronounced like the English *w*:

  Po̲l half (as in kno**w**)
  Vo̲lk wolf (as in kno**w**)
  Bra̲l "he read" (reads as bro**w**)

For better pronunciation, read the following words carefully. If a given letter has several phonetic values, then examples and similar English sounds are given for each.

Slovene Pronunciation Table

Letter	Pronunciation	Symbol
a	car	a
b	1) *end of word*: like p in **p**ut 2) *elsewhere*: like b in **b**ad	p, b
c	Like -ts in ca**ts**	ts
č	**ch**ur**ch**	ch
d	1) *end of word*: like t in sof**t** 2) *elsewhere*: like d in da**d**	t, d
e	b**e**d, f**a**t, th**e**	e, a, eh
f	**f**ar, **ph**iloso**ph**y	f, ph
g	**g**ap	g
h	**h**ouse	h
i	s**ee**, m**ea**l	ee
j	**y**es	y
k	**k**i**ck,** **C**alifornia	c
l	1) *end of word, before a consonant*: like w in bo**w** 2) *elsewhere*: like l in **l**eft	l
m	**M**onday	m
n	**n**orth	n
o	h**o**rn, h**o**t, sh**o**rt	oh
p	**p**lease	o
r	**r**eal, **r**iver	r
s	**s**ix	s
š	**sh**ock	sh
t	**t**axi	t
u	m**oo**n	oo
v	1) *after vowel, before a consonant*: like w in **w**in	w
	2) *alone*: like oo in m**oo**n	oo
	3) *elsewhere*: like v in **v**ery	v
z	**z**ero	z
ž	mea**s**ure	zh

Slovene-English Dictionary

A

a *conj.* but
abecéda *n.f.* alphabet
adíjo *interj.* bye (*fam.*)
administrácija *n.f.* administration
agéncija *n.f.* agency, bureau; **turistična** ~ *n.f.* tourist agency
agènt *n.m.* agent, representative
ajda *n.f.* buckwheat
akademíja *n.f.* academy
akcènt *n.m.* accent
áktovka *n.m.* briefcase
aktuálen *adj.* actual, current, up-to-date
akumulátor *n.m.* car battery
akústičen *adj.* acoustic; **akustična kitara** *n.f.* acoustic guitar
akvárij *n.m.* aquarium
alergíja *n.f.* allergy; **imam alergijo na...** I am allergic to...
álbum *n.m.* album; **foto~** *n.m.* photo album
álga *n.f.* algae, seaweed
ali *conj.* or, either; **greš ~ ne?** are you coming or not?
alkohól *n.m.* alcohol; **~ne pijače** *n.f.pl.* liquor
Alpe *n.f.pl.* Alps; **Julijske** ~ *n.f.pl.* Julian Alps
amatêr *n.m.* amateur
ambasáda *n.f.* embassy
ambasádor *n.m.* ambassador
ambulánta *n.f.* clinic, doctor's office; hospital, health center
àmpak *conj.* but; however
anekdóta *n.f.* anecdote
ángel *n.m.* angel (*relig.*)

ankéta *n.f.* survey, questionnaire, inquiry
ansámbel *n.m.* ensemble, musical group
anténa *n.f.* antenna
antíčen *adj.* antique; aged
antikvariát *n.m.* antique shop
aparát *n.m.* machine, device; piece of equipment
apartmá *n.m.* studio, apartment; ~ **za dve osebi** *n.m.*
   apartment for two
apríl *n.m.* April
arháičen *adj.* archaic
arheológ *n.m.* archaeologist
arhitékt *n.m.* architect
arhitektúra *n.f.* architecture
aróma *n.f.* aroma, scent, fragrance
artičóka *n.f.* artichoke
as *n.m.* ace; champion, winner; **smučarski** ~ *n.m.*
   ski champion
asistènt *n.m.* assistant
aspirín *n.m.* aspirin
ástma *n.f.* asthma
astrologíja *n.f.* astrology
ataše *n.m.* attaché, public servant (*admin.*)
ateíst *n.m.* atheist
átlas *n.m.* atlas
atlétika *n.f.* athletic
atmosfêra *n.f.* atmosphere, setting
aveníja *n.f.* avenue
avgúst *n.m.* August
ávla *n.f.* hall, lobby
avténtičen *adj.* authentic, genuine
ávto(mobil) *n.m.* car, automobile
avtobus *n.m.* bus
avtocesta *n.f.* highway
ávtodom *n.m.* caravan, RV
ávtomehanik *n.m.* mechanic (*autom.*)
ávtor *n.m.* author, creator, writer
avtoritéta *n.f.* authority; power

ávtoštop *n.m.* hitchhiking

azíl *n.m.* asylum

B

bábica *n.f.* grandmother, grandma, granny

bájka *n.f.* story, fairy tale

báker *n.m.* copper

bákla *n.f.* torch

baktérija *n.m.* bacteria, germ

balét *n.m.* ballet

balínanje *n.nt.* bowling; French bocce ball, petanque

balkón *n.m.* balcony

balón *n.m.* balloon

banana *n.f.* banana

bánka *n.f.* bank; **narodna ~** *n.f.* national bank

bánkovec *n.m.* banknote

bar *n.m.* bar, nightclub, pub

barába *n.f.* bastard (*vulg.*)

barantáti *v.* to bargain

bárka *n.f.* (sail)boat

báročen *adj.* baroque; **baročna cerkev** *n.f.* baroque church

barók *n.m.* baroque

barón *n.m.* baron

bárva *n.f.* color

bárvati *v.* to paint, to dye, to tint

básen *n.f.* fable, tale about animals

baterija *n.f.* battery; **žepna ~** *n.f.* flashlight

báti se *v.* to be afraid, to fear

báza *n.f.* base, station (*milt.*)

bazén *n.m.* swimming pool

bazílika *n.f.* basil (*culin.*); basilica (*relig.*)

béda *n.f.* poverty, misery; **živeti v bedi** *v.* to live in poverty

bedák *n.m.* fool, jerk

begúnec *n.m.* refugee
bel *adj.* white; ~ **kruh** *n.m.* white bread
belec *n.m.* white person
beléžiti *v.* to take note
beléžnica *n.f.* notebook, folder
béliti *v.* to paint (*constr.*)
beljakovína *n.f.* protein
belúš *n.m.* asparagus
bencín *n.m.* gasoline, petrol
benéški *adj.* Venetian; ~ **karneval** *n.m.* Venice Carnival
Benétke *n.f.pl.* Venice
beráč *n.m.* beggar
bergla *n.f.* crutch
beséda *n.f.* word
besedni zaklad *n.m.* vocabulary
bésen *adj.* furious, mad
bežáti *v.* to escape, to run away
Bíblija *n.f.* the Bible
bifé *n.m.* snack bar
bíftek *n.m.* steak, beefsteak
bik *n.m.* bull; ~ **oborba** *n.f.* bullfighting
biljard *n.m.* billiard
biografíja *n.f.* biography
bírma *n.f.* communion (*relig.*)
birokracíja *n.f.* bureaucracy
bíser *n.m.* pearl
bíster *adj.* clean, clear; clever, bright, intelligent
bístrica *n.f.* stream, clear water; **Kamniška** ~ *n.f.* Kamnik Stream
bíti *v.* to be
bítje *n.nt.* being; **živo** ~ *n.nt.* living being
bítka *n.f.* battle, fight, struggle
bivalíšče *n.nt.* home, residence
bívanje *n.nt.* staying
bívol *n.m.* buffalo

bívši *adj.* ex-, former; **države bivše Jugoslavije**
n.f.pl. former Yugoslavian countries
blagájna *n.f.* cashbox
blagájničarka *n.f.* cashier, bank clerk
blagó *n.nt.* goods, merchandise
blátnik *n.m.* fender (*autom.*)
bláto *n.nt.* mud
blazína *n.f.* pillow, cushion; **zračna** ~ *n.f.* air mattress
blažílen *adj.* calming, soothing
bled *adj.* pale
blisk *n.m.* lightning, flash
blizu *prep.* close, near; ~ **doma** close to home
bližína *n.f.* closeness, proximity
blížnjica *n.f.* shortcut
blók *n.m.* block; apartment building
blônd *adj.* blond
blúza *n.f.* blouse
bóben *n.m.* drum; **bóbnar** *n.m.* drummer
bodíca *n.m.* thorn, spine
bodóči *adj.* future; ~ **mož** *n.m.* future husband
Bog *n.m.* God; **hvala Bogu!** thank God!
bogástvo *n.nt.* wealth, riches, assets, fortune
bogát *adj.* rich, well-off, wealthy
bogínja *n.f.* goddess
boj *n.m.* battle, fight
boki *n.m.pl.* hips
boks *n.m.* boxing
bolán *adj.* sick, ill, in poor health
boléč *adj.* painful, sore
boleče grlo *n.nt.* sore throat
bolečína *n.f.* ache, pain
bolézen *n.f.* disease, illness, sickness
bôlha *n.f.* flea, bug
bóljši *adj.* better
bólnica, **bolnišnica** *n.f.* hospital
bólničar *n.m.* nurse
bolník *n.m.* patient

bombáž *n.m.* cotton
bombón *n.m.* candy
boríti se *v.* to fight, to struggle
borovníca *n.f.* blueberry; **borovničev sok** *n.m.*
  blueberry juice
bórza *n.f.* stockmarket; **borzni posrednik** *n.m.*
  stockbroker
bos *adj.* barefoot
botáničen *adj.* botanical; **botanični vrt** *n.m.*
  botanical garden
bóter *n.m.* godfather
Božič *n.m.* Christmas; **Božični večer** *n.f.* Christmas
  Eve
bráda *n.f.* beard
bradavíca *n.f.* nipple
brálec *n.m.* reader
braníti *v.* to defend
brat *n.m.* brother; **~ránec** *n.m.* male cousin
bráti *v.* to read
brazgotína *n.f.* scar, mark
bréskev *n.f.* peach
brez *prep.* without; **kava ~ sladkorja** *n.f.* coffee
  without sugar
brezalkohólen *adj.* alcohol-free
brezpláčen *adj.* free of charge, gratis
brezskŕben *adj.* careless
bríga *n.f.* care; **~ me** I don't care; **kaj te ~!** mind
  your own business!
brisáča *n.f.* towel
brísati *v.* to wipe; to mop
bríti *v.* to shave; **pena za britje** *n.f.* aftershave
brítvica *n.f.* razor
brívec *n.m.* barber
bŕki *n.m.pl.* moustache
bron *n.m.* bronze; **~asta medalja** *n.f.* bronze medal
brošúra *n.f.* brochure, booklet
bršljan *n.m.* ivy (*bot.*)

brúhati *v.* to vomit
brúnarica *n.f.* chalet, cabin, hut
búden *adj.* awake, vigilant
budílka *n.f.* alarm clock
búkev *n.f.* beech (*bot.*)
búrja *n.f.* strong wind on the north Adriatic coast

C

car *n.m.* tsar
carína *n.* customs
carinska taksa *n.f.* customs fee
cedílo *n.m.* colander
cel *adj.* whole, entire; ~ **dan** *n.m.* whole day
celína *n.f.* continent
céna *n.f.* price, cost
ceník *n.m.* pricelist, tariff list
cénter *n.m.* center
centiméter *n.m.* centimeter
cépiti *v.* to vaccinate
cérkev *n.f.* church
césta *n.f.* street, road
cestnína *n.f.* toll
cév *n.f.* pipe, tube
cigán *n.m.* gypsy
cigára *n.f.* cigar; **cigaréta** *n.f.* cigarette
cilínder *n.m.* cylinder (*autom.*)
cilj *n.m.* goal, aim; destination; **doseči/zgrešiti** ~ *v.*
    to reach/miss the goal
címet *n.m.* cinnamon
ciprésa *n.f.* cypress (*bot.*)
cirílica *n.f.* Cyrillic (Serbian and Russian alphabet)
církus *n.m.* circus
cmok *n.m.* dumpling; **kruhovi** ~**i** *n.m.pl.* bread
    dumplings
cóna *n.f.* zone, district

copáti *n.m.pl.* slippers
cvet *n.m.* flower; blossom
cvetáča *n.f.* cauliflower
cvétje *n.nt.* flowers; **šopek cvetja** *n.m.* flower bouquet
cvetličár *n.m.* florist
cvréti *v.* to fry

Č

čaj *n.m.* tea; **skodelica ~a** *n.f.* a cup of tea; **čájnik** *n.m.* teapot
čakálnica *n.f.* waiting room
čákati *v.* to wait; **pustiti ~** *v.* to let somebody wait
čarter *n.m.* chartered flight
čas *n.m.* time; **letni ~** *n.m.* season; **od ~a do ~a** from time to time
časopís *n.m.* (daily) newspaper
čast *n.f.* honor; **v ~ mi je** I am honored
čáša *n.f.* wine glass
če *conj.* if, whether
čebéla *n.f.* bee; **čebelárstvo** *n.nt.* apiculture
čebúla *n.f.* onion
čéden *adj.* handsome, good-looking
ček *n.m.* check, cheque; **vnovčiti ~** *v.* to cash a check
čeláda *n.f.* helmet
čeljúst *n.f.* jaw
čêlo *n.nt.* forehead, front; cello (violoncello) (*mus.*)
čep *n.m.* cork, plug
čepráv *conj.* even though, although
česáti *v.* to comb
čêsen *n.m.* garlic; **čêsnova omaka** *n.* garlic sauce
čestítati *v.* to congratulate; **čestítam!** *interj.* congratulations!
čéšnja *n.f.* cherry

četŕt *n.f.* quarter; **ura je ~ čez tri** it's a quarter past three o'clock

četŕtek *n.m.* Thursday

četŕti *num.* fourth

čévelj *n.m.* shoe; **obuti/sezuti si ~** *v.* put on/take off shoes

čevljár *n.m.* shoemaker

čez *prep.* in; across, over; **~ eno leto** in one year's time; **~ cesto** across the street

číli *n.m.* chili

čimprej *prep.* as soon as possible

čipka *n.f.* lace; **Idrijske čipke** *n.f.pl.* Idria laces

čist *adj.* clean, pure, tidy

čistílo *n.nt.* cleanser, detergent; **čistilna krema** *n.f.* cleansing cream

čístiti *v.* to clean

član *n.m.* member; **ustanovni ~** *n.m.* founding member

člának *n.m.* (newspaper) article

člôvek *n.m.* human, man

človéški *adj.* humanlike; **človeška narava** *n.f.* human nature

čokoláda *n.* chocolate; **čokoladna torta** *n.f.* chocolate cake

čoln *n.m.* boat; **motorni ~** *n.m.* motorboat

čopič *n.m.* paintbrush

čŕka *n.f.* letter; **velika ~** *n.f.* capital letter; **mala ~** *n.f.* miniature

čŕkováti *v.* to spell; **lahko črkujete?** can you spell that?

čŕn *adj.* black; **~ a kava** *n.f.* ~ coffee

čŕnec *n.m.* black person

čŕnílo *n.nt.* black ink

čŕta *n.f.* line, stroke

čŕv *n.m.* worm

čtívo *n.nt.* lecture

čúden *adj.* odd, strange, weird

čúdež *n.m.* miracle
čudovít *adj.* wonderful
čústvo *n.nt.* emotion, feeling
čut *n.m.* sense
čutiti *v.* to feel, to sense
čuvaj *n.m.* guard, security
čvrst *adj.* firm, hard, strong

D

da *interj.* for, to; **prišel sem, ~ bi pomagal** I came
 to help
dáleč *prep.* far; **od ~** *prep.* from far away
dáljnji *adj.* far, remote, distant; **~ sorodniki** *n.m.pl.*
 distant relatives
daljnoglèd *n.m.* field glass, telescope
dáma *n.f.* lady; draughts
dan *n.m.* day; **dober ~!** *interj.* hello!; **rojstni ~** *n.m.*
 birthday
dánes *adv.* today; **katerega smo ~?** which date is
 today?; **~ zvečer** *adv.* tonight
darílo *n.nt.* gift, present
dáti *v.* to give; **~ v najem** *v.* to rent out
dátum *n.m.* date; **današnji ~** *n.m.* today's date
dávek *n.m.* duty, tax; **~ na dodano vrednost
 (D.D.V.)** *n.m.* V.A.T.
dêbel *adj.* fat, overweight; thick; **prodaja na
 debelo** *n.f.* retail, wholesale
dêblo *n.nt.* trunk (*bot.*)
decémber *n.m.* December
déček *n.m.* boy
dédek *n.m.* grandfather, grandpa
dédič *n.m.* heir, inheritor; **dédiščina** *n.f.* heritage,
 inheritance
defékt *n.m.* defect, flaw
dejávnost *n.f.* activity

déjstvo *n.nt.* fact, information

deklè *n.nt.* girl

del *n.m.* part, piece; **sprednji/ zadnji** ~ *n.m.* front/back part

délati *v.* to do, to work; ~ **se** *v.* to pretend; **kaj delaš?** what are you doing?

délavec *n.m.* worker, employee; **delávnica** *n.f.* workshop; workplace

délen *adj.* partial

délež *n.m.* fraction, portion, share

delfín *n.m.* dolphin

delikatésa *n.f.* delicatessen

delíti *v.* to share, to split

delnica *n.f.* share, stock; **delničar** *n.m.* shareholder

délo *n.nt.* work; **delovni čas** *n.m.* working hours

delováti *v.* to work, to function

demokracíja *n.f.* democracy

denár *n.m.* cash, money; ~**nica** *n.f.* wallet

desèt *num.* ten

desêti *num.* tenth

deskà *n.f.* board; **deskanje na vodi/snegu** *n.nt.* surfing/snowboarding

désno *adj.* right; **desnica** *n.f.* right hand

devét *num.* nine

devêti *num.* ninth

devíza *n.f.* foreign currency

dež *n.m.* rain

dežêla *n.f.* country; **živeti na deželi** *v.* to live in the countryside

deževáti *v.* to rain

dežník *n.m.* umbrella

dežúren *adj.* on duty; **dežurna lekarna** *n.f.* 24-hour pharmacy

diagnóza *n.f.* diagnosis

dialékt *n.m.* dialect

diamant *n.m.* diamond

diaréja *n.f.* diarrhea

diéta *n.f.* diet; **sem na dieti** I am on a diet

díhati *v.* to breathe, to respire

dim *n.m.* smoke; **~nik** *n.m.* chimney

dinámo *n.m.* dynamo (*autom.*)

diplóma *n.f.* diploma

diplomát *n.m.* diplomat

diréktor *n.m.* director, chairman, boss (*bus.*)

dirigènt *n.m.* bandmaster, choir director

dírka *n.f.* race; **~ ti** *v.* to race

dišáti *v.* to smell

divjáčina *n.f.* game (*culin.*)

dívji *adj.* wild, untamed; uncultivated (*bot.*)

dlan *n.f.* palm

dnevnik *n.m.* news, journal; diary

dnevno *adj.* daily; **dnevni časopis** *n.m.* daily
newspaper

dno *n.m.* bottom

do *prep.* until; **~ kdaj?** until when?; **od treh ~ petih**
from three to five

doba *n.f.* age, time period

dóber *adj.* good, well

dobíti *v.* to get, to obtain, to gain

dobrodošli! *interj.* welcome!

dodatek *n.m.* addition, supplement, extra

dodáti *v.* to add; to append

dogájati se *v.* to be happening; **kaj se dogaja?**
what is happening?

dogódek *n.m.* event, incident

dogôvor *n.m.* agreement, deal, settlement

dohódek *n.m.* income, wage

dojênček *n.m.* baby, infant

dójka *n.f.* breast

dokàz *n.m.* proof, evidence; **zaradi nezadostnih
dokazov** due to insufficient evidence

doklèr *prep.* until

dóktor *n.m.* doctor; **~ prava** *n.m.* Doctor of Law

dokumènt *n.m.* document; **dokumentarni film**
n.m. documentary
dol *prep.* down; **iti ~** *v.* to go down(stairs)
dólar *n.m.* dollar; **ameriški ~** *n.* American dollar;
kanadski ~ *n.* Canadian dollar
dolg *adj.* long; *n.m.* debt
dólgčas *n.m.* boredom; **dolgočásiti se** *v.* to be bored
dolgotrájen *adj.* long-lasting, durable
dolína *n.f.* valley
dolžnóst *n.f.* duty, obligation
dom *n.m.* home
domáč *adj.* home, homemade; domestic; **domače**
živali *n.f.pl.* pets
domačín *n.m.* native, inhabitant
domišljíja *n.f.* imagination
domotóžje *n.m.* homesickness
domovína *n.f.* home country
Donava *n.f.* Danube (river)
dopóldne *prep.* before noon, late morning (A.M.)
dopólniti *v.* to complete; to upgrade
dopúst *n.m.* holiday, vacation
doséči *v.* to achieve
dostáviti *v.* to deliver; **dostava hrane** *n.f.* food
delivery
dostôp *n.m.* access; **~en** *adj.* accessible,
approachable
dotíkati se *v.* to touch
dovóliti *v.* to permit, to allow
dovòlj *prep.* enough
dovoljênje *n.nt.* license, permission
dóza *n.f.* dose
drag *adj.* expensive, costly, dear; **predrago** *adj.* too
expensive
dragocén *adj.* precious, expensive; **~ kamen** *n.m.*
precious stone
dragúlj *n.m.* jewel
dráma *n.f.* drama

drevó *n.nt.* tree

dróbec *n.m.* bit, small piece

drobíti *v.* to crush; **drobljen led** *n.m.* crushed ice

drobíž *n.m.* change, small money

drog *n.m.* bar, pole, rod

dróga *n.f.* drug

drsalíšče *n.nt.* skating rink

drˊsati *v.* to (ice) skate; **umetnostnjo drsanje** *n.nt.* figure skating

drúg *num.* second, (an) other; **~ za drugim** one behind the other

drugáčen *adj.* different

drúgič *adv.* second time, another time

drugjé *adv.* elsewhere, away

drúštvo *n.nt.* association, organization

drúžba *n.f.* company, group; **v družbi prijateljev** in the company of friends

drúž(a)ben *adj.* social; **družbene vede** *n.f.pl.* social sciences

družína *n.f.* family

drˊva *n.f.pl.* firewood

držáti *v.* to hold; **~ besedo** *v.* to keep one's word; **drži se!** hold on!; **drži!** it's a deal!

držáva *n.f.* country, state

držáven *adj.* state, government; **državna blagajna** *n.f.* state treasury

državlján *n.m.* citizen; **Slovensko ~stvo** *n.nt.* Slovene citizenship

dúcat *n.m.* dozen

duhovít *adj.* funny, amusing

duhóvnik *n.m.* priest

Dúnaj *n.m.* Vienna; **~ski zrezek** *n.m.* Vienna steak

dúša *n.f.* soul

dva, dve *num.* two

dvájset *num.* twenty

dvákrat *num.* twice

dvigálo *n.m.* elevator

dvójčka *n.m.pl.* twins
dvójen *adj.* double
dvojezíčen *adj.* bilingual
dvojína *n.f.* dual (*gram.*)
dvom *n.m.* doubt; **brez ~a** without a doubt
dvorána *n.f.* hall; **sodna ~** *n.f.* court
dvoríšče *n.nt.* yard, backyard
dvožívka *n.f.* amphibian
džip *n.m.* jeep, four-wheel drive

E

êden *num.* one; **~ izmed njih** one of them
ednína *n.f.* singular
ekípa *n.f.* team
ekonomíja *n.f.* economy; **ekonomist** *n.m.* economist
ekonomski *adj.* economical
ekskúrzija *n.f.* excursion
ekspêrt *n.m.* expert, specialist
eksprésen *adj.* express
elástičen *adj.* elastic, stretchy
elástika *n.f.* elastic, rubber band
eléktričar *n.m.* electrician; **eléktrični tok** *n.m.*
    electric current
eléktrika *n.f.* electricity
emigrácija *n.f.* emigration
en, ena, eno *num.* one; **eno pivo, prosim~** one beer,
    please!
enájst *num.* eleven
enák *adj.* equal, identical, the same
enáko *prep.* same, equal; **hvala ~!** likewise!
enciklopedíja *n.f.* encyclopedia
energíja *n.f.* energy, power
ênkrat *num.* once; **še ~** once again; **~ za vselej** once
    and for all
enostáven *adj.* simple

enôta *n.f.* unit, division (*milt.*)
éter *n.m.* ether
etikéta *n.f.* label, sticker
Evrópa *n.f.* Europe; **Evropska unija** *n.f.* European
   Union

F

faktúra *n.f.* invoice, bill
fakultéta *n.f.* faculty; **Pravna** ~ *n.f.* Law Faculty
fant *n.m.* boy, young man
fantazíja *n.f.* fantasy, imagination
fašízem *n.m.* fascism
fazán *n.m.* pheasant
fébruar *n.m.* February
fíga *n.f.* fig
film *n.m.* movie; **vrteti** ~ *v.* play a movie
filozóf *n.m.* philosopher; **filozofíja** *n.f.* philosophy
fílter *n.m.* filter
fin *adj.* fine, excellent
fináncе *n.f.pl.* capital, finances; **Ministrstvo za** ~
   n.nt. Ministry of Finances
fízika *n.f.* physics
fížol *n.m.* beans
flávta *n.f.* flute
folklóra *n.f.* folklore
fonétika *n.f.* phonetics
formálen *adj.* formal, official; **formálnost** *n.f.*
   formality
formát *n.m.* format, layout
fotoaparát *n.m.* camera
fotográf *n.m.* photographer; **fotografíja** *n.f.* photo
fotografírati *v.* to take photos
fotográfski *adj.* photographic
frank *n.m.* franc; **švicarski** ~ Swiss franc
fráza *n.f.* phrase

fréska *n.f.* fresco
frizêr *n.f.* hairdresser; **frizúra** *n.f.* hairdo
funkcionírati *v.* to function, to work

G

galeb *n.m.* seagull
galérija *n.f.* gallery; **umetnostna** ~ *n.f.* art gallery
galóna *n.f.* gallon (3.78 liters)
garancíja *n.f.* warranty, guarantee
garáža *n.m.* garage
garderóba *n.f.* wardrobe
gasílec *n.m.* fireman
gasíti *v.* to extinguish; ~ **požar** *v.* to put out a fire
generálen *adj.* general; **generalni director** *n.m.*
   head director
geografíja *n.f.* geography
geologíja *n.f.* geology
gêslo *n.m.* password
gimnástika *n.f.* gymnastic
gimnázija *n.f.* lyceum, high school; **klasična** ~ *n.f.*
   classical lyceum
ginekológ *n.m.* gynecologist
gládek *adj.* smooth, sleek
glágol *n.m.* verb; **nepravilni** ~ *n.m.* irregular verb
   (*gram.*)
glas *n.m.* voice; **govoriti na** ~ *v.* talking loud
glásba *n.f.* music
glasbeni *adj.* musical; **glasbena oddaja** *n.f.*
   musical show
glásbenik *n.m.* musician
glásen *adj.* loud; **pre~** *adj.* too loud
gláva *n.f.* head; **glavoból** *n.m.* headache
gláven *adj.* main; **glavno mesto** *n.nt.* capital (city)
glavník *n.m.* comb

gledálci *n.m.pl.* viewers, audience

gledalíšče *n.m.* theater; **gledališki igralec** *n.m.* theater performer

glédati *v.* to watch, to look (at)

gléženj *n.m.* ankle; **zlomljen ~** *n.m.* broken ankle

glína *n.f.* clay

globína *n.f.* depth, profundity

globòk *adj.* deep, profound

glodálec *n.m.* gnawer; rodent (*zool.*)

gluh *adj.* deaf; **~ oném** *adj.* deaf-mute

gnéča *n.f.* crowd, throng

gnézdo *n.nt.* nest

gnil *adj.* rotten; **~ o jabolko** *n.nt.* rotten apple

góba *n.f.* mushroom; **užitna/strupena ~** *n.f.* edible/poisonous mushroom

gól *n.m.* goal, score

gòl *adj.* naked, nude

gólaž *n.m.* goulash

golf *n.m.* golf; **mini ~** *n.m.* miniature golf

golób *n.m.* pigeon

gor *prep.* up; **po stopnicah ~** *prep.* up the stairs

gôra *n.f.* mountain; **v gorah** *prep.* in the mountains

gorčíca *n.f.* mustard

goréti *v.* to burn, to be on fire

gori! *interj.* fire!

gorívo *n.nt.* fuel, energy

gos *n.f.* goose

gosenica *n.f.* caterpillar

gospá *n.f.* Miss, Madame; **ga.** *n.f.* Mrs.

gospód *n.m.* Mister; **g.** *n.m.* Mr.

gospodár *n.m.* landlord

gospodárstvo *n.nt.* economy; **državno ~** *n.nt.* state economy

gospodínja *n.f.* housewife; housekeeper

gòst *adj.* dense, thick

gôst *n.m.* guest, visitor

gostílna *n.f.* restaurant, inn
gostíti *v.* to host
gostoljúbnost *n.m.* hospitality
gotòv *adj.* done, finished, ready, sure
gotovína *n.f.* cash, ready money; **gotovínski**
popust *n.m.* cash discount
govédina *n.f.* beef; **goveja juha** *n.f.* beef soup
góvor *n.m.* speech; **imeti ~** *v.* to have a speech
govoríti *v.* to talk, to speak; **~ po slovensko** *v.* to
speak Slovene; **tiho ~** *v.* to talk quietly
gozd *n.m.* forest, wood
grad *n.m.* castle
gradíti *v.* to build, to construct
grah *n.m.* peas
gram *n.m.* gram
gramofon *n.m.* gramophone, phonograph
grb *n.m.* blazon
grd *adj.* ugly; **~o vreme** *n.nt.* bad weather; **~**
ravnati z nekom *v.* to treat somebody poorly
grênek *adj.* bitter
grenívka *n.f.* grapefruit
grétje *n.nt.* heating
gríč *n.m.* hill, mount
grípa *n.f.* flu
grísti *v.* to bite
gŕlo *n.nt.* throat
grm *n.m.* bush, shrub; **~ ičevje** *n.nt.* bushes
grôb *n.m.* grave, tomb
grób *adj.* harsh, raw, untreated
grof *n.m.* count; **Celjski ~je** *n.m.pl.* the Celje Counts
grom *n.m.* thunder
grôza *n.f.* horror, terror; **grozljivka** *n.f.* horror movie
grózdje *n.nt.* grape
grúča *n.f.* bunch, group
gúma *n.f.* gum, rubber
gumb *n.m.* button, key, knob

H

h/k *prep.* to, at; **grem ~ Katji** I am going to Katja's place

haló *interj.* hello (*tel.*)

hamburger *n.m.* hamburger

harmónika *n.f.* harmonica

hčér, hčerka *n.f.* daughter

hektár *n.m.* hectare

helikópter *n.m.* helicopter

herój *n.m.* hero

higiéna *n.f.* hygiene

hímna *n.f.* anthem, hymn

hinávec *n.m.* hypocrite

híša *n.f.* house; **dvonadstropna ~** *n.f.* two-story house

híter *adj.* fast, quick

hitéti *v.* to hurry, to rush

hitróst *n.f.* speed

hkráti *adv.* at the same time

hláče *n.f.pl.* pants, trousers; **kratke ~** *n.f.pl.* short pants

hlad *n.m.* cool, coolness, fresh(ness); **~en** *adj.* cool; **~ílnik** *n.m.* refrigerator

hlev *n.m.* stable

hodíti *v.* to walk; to hike; **~ peš v šolo** *v.* to walk to school

hodník *n.m.* corridor, hall, passage

hókej *n.m.* hockey; **~ na ledu** *n.m.* ice hockey

homoseksuálec *n.m.* homosexual

hormón *n.m.* hormone

hotél *n.m.* hotel; **hotelski gost** *n.m.* hotel guest

hotéti *v.* to want

hrána *n.f.* food; **domača ~** *n.f.* homemade food; **hitra ~** *n.f.* fast food

hrániti *v.* to feed; keep, to save

hrast *n.m.* oak

hŕbet *n.m.* back, backside; **obrniti ~ nekomu** *v.* to turn one's back on sbd

hrbteníca *n.f.* spine
hren *n.m.* horseradish
hrib *n.m.* hill
hrošč *n.m.* bug
hrup *n.m.* noise
hrúška *n.f.* pear; pear tree
hud *adj.* mad, angry, upset; ~ **pes** *n.m.* dangerous dog
hújšati *v.* to be on a diet
humanitáren *adj.* humanitarian; **humanitarna**
    pomoč *n.f.* humanitarian aid
humór *n.m.* humor; **smisel za** ~ *n.m.* sense of humor
hvála *interj.* thank you, thanks; **najlepša** ~ thank
    you very much
hvaléžen *adj.* grateful, thankful

I

idéja *n.f.* idea
identificírati *v.* to identify, to recognize
identitéta *n.f.* identity
ideologíja *n.f.* ideology
idíličen *adj.* idyllic
idiót *n.m.* jerk, idiot (*vulg.*)
ígla *n.f.* needle; ~ **za pletenje** *n.f.* knitting needle
ígra *n.f.* game; **olimpijske igre** *n.f.pl.* Olympic Games
igráča *n.f.* toy
igrálec *n.m.* player; **gledališki** ~ *n.m.* theater actor;
    igralnica *n.f.* casino
igráti *v.* to play; to act (*theat.*); ~ **šah** *v.* to play
    chess; ~ **trobento** *v.* to play the trumpet
ilustrácija *n.f.* illustration, drawing
imé *n.nt.* first name; **dekliško** ~ *n.nt.* maiden name;
    kako ti je ~**?** what is your name?
imeník *n.m.* name list; white pages (*tel.*)
imenovati (se) *v.* to name (oneself); **imenujem se**
    Alice my name is Alice

iméti *v.* to have; ~ **rad** *v.* to like; **lepo se imejte!** have a nice time!

iméti rájši *v.* to prefer

imigrácija *n.f.* immigration

impérij *n.m.* empire; **Rimski** ~ *n.m.* Roman Empire

impresioním *n.m.* impressionism

improvizírati *v.* to improvise

in *conj.* and

industríja *n.f.* industry; **težka** ~ *n.f.* heavy industry

infárkt *n.m.* heart attack

informácija *n.f.* information, data

íngver *n.m.* ginger; **~jevo pivo** *n.nt.* ginger beer

injékcija *n.f.* injection, syringe

inozémstvo *n.m.* foreign land

instínkt *n.m.* instinct, gut feeling

instrumènt *n.m.* instrument; **glasbeni** ~ *n.m.* musical instrument

inštitút *n.m.* institute; ~ **slovenskega jezika** *n.m.* Slovene language institute

inštrúktor *n.m.* instructor

intelektuálec *n.m.* intellectual

inteligénten *adj.* intelligent

interés *n.m.* interest

intervjú *n.m.* interview

intímen *adj.* intimate, private

invalíd *n.m.* invalid, disabled person

inženír *n.m.* engineer

iskáti *v.* to look for, to search, to seek

ískra *n.f.* spark

íslam *n.m.* Islam

ísti *adj.* the same; **istočasno** *adv.* at the same time

Ístra *n.f.* Istra; **Hrvaška** ~ *n.f.* Croatian Istra

itd. (in tako dalje) *adv.* etc. (et cetera)

íti *v.* to go; ~ **na sprehod** *v.* to take a walk

iz *prep.* from; **prihaja** ~ **Sarajeva** he is coming from Sarajevo

izbíra *n.f.* choice, selection

izbóljšati *v.* to improve
izbrati *v.* to choose, to pick, to select
izčŕpen *adj.* comprehensive
izdátek *n.m.* expense, disbursement
izdélati *v.* to make, to produce
izdélek *n.m.* product, item
izgíniti *v.* to disappear
izgléd *n.m.* appearance
izglédati *v.* to appear; **dobro izgledaš** you look well
izgovorjáva *n.f.* pronunciation
izgubíti (se) *v.* to lose (oneself)
izhòd *n.m.* exit, way out
izíd *n.m.* result
izjáva *n.f.* declaration, statement
izkáznica *n.f.* card; **članska ~** *n.f.* member's card
izklópiti *v.* to turn off, to switch off
izkŕcati se *v.* to disembark
izkúšnja *n.f.* experience
izlèt *n.m.* trip, excursion
izlóžba *n.f.* display, shop window
izmenjava *n.f.* exchange; **študentska ~** *n.f.* student
    exchange
izmériti *v.* to measure
izobrázba *n.f.* education; **izobrážen** *adj.* educated
izpít *n.m.* examination, test
izpod *prep.* from beneath
izpólniti *v.* to fulfill, to carry out
izposóditi (si) *v.* to borrow
izprázniti *v.* to empty
izpustíti *v.* to release, to drop, to set free
izrábiti *v.* to take advantage, to make use; **~ priložnost**
    v. to take the opportunity
izračúnati *v.* to calculate
izràz *n.m.* expression, term; **strokovni ~** *n.m.*
    professional term
izročílo *n.nt.* tradition; **ustno ~** *n.nt.* oral transmission
izstopíti *v.* to step out, to get out/off

izúm *n.m.* invention, discovery
izvédeti *v.* to learn, to find out
izven *prep.* out of, outside of; ~ **mesta** *prep.* out of town
izvijáč *n.m.* screwdriver
izvír *n.m.* source; spring
izvíren *adj.* original; **izvirno besedilo** *n.nt.* original text
izvòd *n.m.* copy
izvólite! *interj.* here it is!
izvòr *n.m.* origin; root; source
izvòz *n.m.* export
izvŕsten *adj.* excellent, superb

J

ja *adv.* yes
jáblana *n.f.* apple tree
jábolko *n.nt.* apple; **jabolčni zavitek** *n.m.* apple pie; **jabolčnik** *n.m.* cider
Jádran *n.m.* Adriatic Sea; masculine name
jádrati *v.* to sail, to navigate
jádro *n.nt.* sail; **razpeti** ~ *v.* to set sail
jágnje *n.nt.* lamb
jágoda *n.f.* strawberry
jáhati *v.* to ride; go horseback riding
jáhta *n.f.* yacht
jájce *n.nt.* egg; **trdo/mehko kuhano** ~ *n.nt.* hard-/soft-boiled egg
jájčevec *n.m.* eggplant
jákost *n.f.* volume
jáma *n.f.* pit, cave
jánež *n.m.* anise
jánuar *n.m.* January
járd *n.m.* yard (0.914 m)
jásen *adj.* clear, bright; evident

jástog *n.m.* crayfish, lobster

jáven *adj.* public, open; **javno mnenje** *n.nt.* public opinion

jávnost *n.f.* public

jávor *n.m.* maple

jázbec *n.m.* badger

jazz *n.m.* jazz

je *v.* is (3rd *person*; *verb to be*)

jed *n.f.* dish, meal; **narodna ~** *n.f.* national dish

jedílnica *n.f.* dining room

jêklo *n.nt.* steel

jêlen *adj.* stag, hart

jélka *n.f.* fir tree

jesén *n.f.* autumn; **~ski** *adj.* autumn

jésti *v.* to eat

jetra *n.f.pl.* liver; **jetrna pašteta** *n.f.* liver pâté

jéza *n.f.* anger, rage

jézen *adj.* angry, furious, mad

jézero *n.nt.* lake

jêzik *n.m.* language; tongue; **tuj ~** *n.m.* foreign language

jezíti se *v.* to be angry

jež *n.m.* hedgehog; **morski ~** *n.m.* sea urchin

jod *n.m.* iodine

jógurt *n.m.* yogurt; **sadni ~** *n.m.* fruit yogurt

jok *n.m.* crying, weeping; **jókati** *v.* to cry, to weep

jópič *n.f.* jacket

jug *n.m.* south; **na ~u** *adv.* in the south

júha *n.f.* soup; broth; **goveja ~** *n.f.* beef soup

júlij *n.m.* July

junák *n.m.* hero; **glavni ~** *n.m.* protagonist, main actor (*cin.*)

júnij *n.m.* June

jútri *adv.* tomorrow; **~ zjutraj/zvečer** *adv.* tomorrow morning/evening

jútro *n.nt.* morning; **dobro ~!** *interj.* good morning!

júžen *adj.* southern; **južni tečaj** *n.m.* South Pole

K

k/h *prep.* to, at; **pridi ~ meni** come to me
kábel *n.m.* cable; **kabelska televizija** *n.f.* cable TV
kabína *n.f.* cabin; **telefonska ~** *n.f.* phone booth
káča *n.f.* snake, serpent
kád *n.f.* (bath)tub
kàdar *conj.* when
kadílec *n.m.* smoker
kadíti *v.* to smoke; **~ prepovedano** no smoking
kaj *pron.* what; **~ je?** what is it?
kakao *n.m.* cocoa
kakó *adv.* how; **~ gre?** how is it going? **~ daleč je?**
how far is it?
kàkor *conj.* as; **~ hitro mogoče** as soon as possible
kakóvost *n.f.* quality
kákšen *adv.* how; **na ~ način?** in what way?
káktus *n.m.* cactus
kálcij *n.m.* calcium
kalórija *n.f.* calorie
kam *conj.* where; **~ greš?** where are you going?
kaméla *n.f.* camel
kámen *n.m.* stone, rock; **ledvični ~** *n.m.* kidney stone
kamílice *n.f.pl.* chamomile
kamín *n.m.* fireplace
kamión *n.m.* truck
kanál *n.m.* canal, channel; **Sueški ~** *n.m.* Suez Canal
kandidát *n.m.* candidate, applicant
kanú *n.m.* canoe
káos *n.m.* chaos, confusion
kap *n.f.* stroke; **srčna ~** *n.f.* heart attack
kápa *n.f.* cap, hood
kapéla *n.f.* chapel (*relig.*)
kapétan *n.m.* captain
kapitál *n.m.* capital, funds; **vložiti ~** *v.* to invest money
kapitalízem *n.m.* capitalism
káplja *n.f.* drop; **po kapljah** by drops

kapník *n.m.* stalactite

kapúca *n.f.* hood

karákter *n.f.* character; ~ **ístika** *n.f.* characteristic, feature

karamból *n.m.* (car) crash

kariêra *n.f.* career

karnevál *n.f.* carnival

kárta *n.f.* cart, map, ticket; **igrati karte** *v.* to play cards; **kartotéka** *n.f.* file

kaséta *n.f.* tape

kasnéje *adv.* later

káša *n.f.* porridge

kášljati *v.* to cough

katalóg *n.m.* catalog; **prodajni** ~ *n.* sales catalog

katedrála *n.f.* cathedral

kategoríja *n.f.* category, class

katéri *adv.* which; **katerega smo danes?** which date is today?

kátering *n.m.* catering

katólik *n.m.* Catholic; **Katoliška cerkev** *n.f.* Catholic church

káva *n.f.* coffee; **črna** ~ *n.f.* black coffee; **bela** ~ *n.f.* chicory coffee

kavalír *n.m.* gentleman

kavárna *n.f.* coffeehouse, café

kávbojke *n.f.pl.* jeans

kávč *n.m.* sofa

kazálec *n.m.* indicator; index finger

kazálo *n.nt.* index, table of contents

kazáti *v.* to show, to point at

kázen *n.f.* punishment, penalty

kdaj *adv.* when; ~ **pa** ~ every now and then

kdo *pron.* who

kémičen *adj.* chemical; **kemična čistilnica** *n.f.* dry cleaner

kemíja *n.f.* chemistry; **organska** ~ *n.f.* organic chemistry

kémik *n.m.* chemist

ker *conj.* because, as

kerámika *n.f.* ceramics

ki *conj.* who, which, that; **fant ~ bere** the boy who reads

kíhati *v.* to sneeze

kilográm *n.m.* kilogram

kilométer *n.m.* kilometer

kilovát *n.m.* kilowatt

kíno, kinematográf *n.m.* movie theater

kiósk *n.m.* kiosk, newsstand

kip *n.m.* statue, sculpture; **~ ar** *n.m.* sculptor

kirúrg *n.m.* surgeon; **~ íja** *n.f.* surgery

kis *n.m.* vinegar

kísel *adj.* sour, acid; **kíslo zelje** *n.nt.* sauerkraut

kisík *n.m.* oxygen

kit *n.m.* whale

kitára *n.f.* guitar; **električna/akustična ~** *n.f.* electric/acoustic guitar

kje *adv.* where

kladívo *n.nt.* hammer

klánec *n.m.* uphill

klarinét *n.m.* clarinet

klásičen *adj.* classical

klavír *n.m.* piano

klepetáti *v.* to chat, to chitchat

kléšče *n.f.pl.* tongs

klet *n.f.* basement, cellar; **vinska ~** *n.f.* wine cellar

klic *n.m.* call, shout; **telefonski ~** *n.m.* phone call

klicáti *v.* to call; **pokliči me!** call me!

klièent *n.m.* client, customer

klíma *n.f.* climate; **~tska naprava** *n.f.* air-conditioning

klínika *n.f.* clinic, clinical hospital

kljub *conj.* in spite of, despite

ključ *n.m.* key; **~avnica** *n.f.* lock

kljun *n.m.* bill, peak (*zool.*)

klobása *n.f.* sausage; **Kranjska ~** *n.f.* Carniolan
  sausage
klobúk *n.m.* hat
klòp *n.m.* tick (*zool.*)
klóp *n.f.* bench, seat
klub *n.m.* club
kmálu *adv.* soon, shortly
kmet *n.m.* farmer, peasant; **kmečki turizem** *n.m.*
  rural tourism
kmetíja *n.f.* farm, farmhouse; **kmetíjstvo** *n.nt.*
  agriculture, farming
knjíga *n.f.* book; **kuharska ~** *n.f.* cookbook;
  knjigárna *n.f.* bookshop
knjižévnost *n.f.* literature
knjížnica *n.f.* library
ko *conj.* when; as
kócka *n.f.* cube, dice; **ledena ~** *n.f.* ice cube; **~ti** *v.*
  to gamble
kóča *n.f.* cottage, hut, cabin
kočíja *n.f.* carriage
kokóš *n.f.* hen
kóktajl *n.m.* cocktail
koledár *n.m.* calendar
kôlek *n.m.* stamp (*admin.*)
kolendár *n.m.* calendar
koléno *n.nt.* knee
kolésar *n.m.* (bi)cyclist; **kolesariti** *v.* to (bi)cycle
kolíčina *n.f.* amount, quantity
kóliko *adv.* how; **~krat** *adv.* how many times
koló *n.nt.* bike, bicycle; wheel; **~voz** *n.m.* lane
kolodvór *n.m.* railway station
kómaj *adv.* barely, hardly; just
komár *n.m.* mosquito
kómbi *n.m.* van
kombinácija *n.f.* combination
komédija *n.f.* comedy
komerciálen *adj.* commercial

komisíja *n.f.* commission
komólec *n.m.* elbow
kompromís *n.m.* compromise
komunikácija *n.f.* communication
komunízem *n.m.* communism
koncêrt *n.m.* concert
končáti *v.* to finish, to end
kondóm *n.m.* condom
kônec *n.m.* end, conclusion, finish
konferénca *n.f.* conference
kongrés *n.m.* congress
koníca *n.f.* point, top
konj *n.m.* horse
kónjak *n.m.* cognac
konstitúcija *n.f.* constitution
kontinènt *n.m.* continent
kontracépcija *n.f.* contraception
kontróla *n.f.* control, supervision, verification
konzêrva *n.m.* can, tin; **konzervirano sadje** *n.nt.*
    canned fruit
kónzul *n.m.* consul; **~ at** *n.m.* consulate
kopalíšče *n.nt.* swimming pool
kopálke *n.f.pl.* swimsuit
kopálnica *n.f.* bathroom
kopáti *v.* to dig, to excavate
kópati (se) *v.* to bathe
kopél *n.f.* bath; **zdravilna ~** *n.f.* healing bath
kópija *n.f.* copy
kôpno *n.nt.* land, mainland
kopríva *n.f.* nettle (*bot.*)
korák *n.m.* step, pace
korenína *n.f.* root
korênje *n.nt.* carrot
korespondénca *n.f.* correspondence
koríst *n.f.* advantage, use, benefit
korísten *adj.* useful, profitable

korúza *n.f.* corn; **koruzni kruh** *n.m.* cornbread
kos *n.m.* piece, slice; **kóšček** *n.m.* small piece, bit
kosílo *n.nt.* lunch
kósiti *v.* to lunch
kosmíči *n.m.pl.* cereals
kost *n.f.* bone
kôstanj *n.m.* chestnuts; **pečen** ~ *n.m.* baked chestnut
kostúm *n.m.* costume, outfit
koš *n.m.* basket; ~ **za smeti** *n.m.* dustbin, garbage
    can; ~ **árka** *n.f.* basketball
košát *adj.* branch-filled; bushy; rich
kót *n.m.* angle, corner
kot *conj.* as, than; ~ **ponavadi...** as usual...
kotálkati se *v.* to skate
kovánec *n.m.* coin
kóvček *n.m.* suitcase
kovína *n.f.* metal
kôza *n.f.* goat; **kozji sir** *n.m.* goat cheese
kozárec *n.m.* glass, cup
kozmétika *n.f.* cosmetic
kozoróg *n.m.* capricorn
kóža *n.f.* skin; **kožna alergija** *n.f.* skin allergy
kradljívec *n.m.* thief
kràj *n.m.* place, spot; **rojstni** ~ *n.m.* birthplace
krajéven *adj.* local; **krajevni klic** *n.m.* local phone
    call
kralj *n.m.* king; **~ica** *n.f.* queen; ~ **évski** *adj.* royal
Kras *n.m.* Karst
krásti *v.* to steal, to rob
kraški kamen *n.m.* limestone rock
krátek *adj.* brief, short; **pred kratkim** *prep.* recently
kráva *n.f.* cow
kraváta *n.f.* tie
kréda *n.f.* chalk; crayon
kredít *n.m.* credit; ~ **na kartica** *n.f.* credit card
kréker *n.m.* cracker

kréma *n.f.* cream; **sončna ~** *n.f.* sunscreen; **zobna ~** *n.f.* toothpaste

krémpelj *n.m.* claw; clutch (*zool.*)

krêpek *adj.* strong, robust

kŕhek *adj.* brittle, fragile

kri *n.f.* blood; **krvna skupina** *n.f.* blood group

kričáti *v.* to shout, to scream

kríket *n.m.* cricket

krílo *n.nt.* wing; skirt (*cloth.*)

kristál *n.m.* crystal

kristján *n.m.* Christian

krítik *n.m.* critic, reviewer

kriv *adj.* guilty, culpable

krivíca *n.f.* injustice, wrong

krivúlja *n.f.* curve

kríza *n.f.* crisis

križ *n.m.* cross, crucifix; **~anka** *n.f.* crossword puzzle

križarjenje *n.nt.* cruise

križíšče *n.nt.* crossroad, crossing

krmílo *n.nt.* rudder, wheel (*autom.*)

kŕmiti *v.* to feed (*zool.*)

krôf *n.m.* doughnut

krog *n.m.* circle

krojáč *n.m.* tailor

krokodíl *n.m.* crocodile

krompír *n.m.* potato

króna *n.f.* crown

króžnik *n.m.* plate; **globok ~** *n.m.* soup dish

krst *n.m.* baptism (*relig.*)

krščánstvo *n.nt.* Catholicism

krt *n.m.* mole

krtáča *n.f.* brush

kruh *n.m.* bread; **štruca ~ a** *n.f.* loaf of bread; **popečen ~** *n.m.* toast

kŕzno *n.nt.* fur

kubíčen *adj.* cubic; **kubični meter** *n.m.* cubic meter

kuhálnik *n.m.* cooker, stove; **plinski** ~ *n.m.* gas stove
kúhar *n.m.* cook
kúhati *v.* to cook
kúhinja *n.f.* kitchen
kúkavica *n.f.* cuckoo
kultúra *n.f.* culture; **kulturno društvo** *n.nt.* cultural
   association
kúmara *n.f.* cucumber; pickle
kupčíja *n.f.* bargain, business, deal
kupè *n.m.* train compartment
kúpec *n.m.* buyer, purchaser
kúpiti *v.* to buy, to purchase
kupón *n.m.* coupon
kurír *n.m.* courier; **~ska služba** *n.f.* courier service
kurjáva *n.f.* heating, warming; **centralna** ~ *n.f.*
   central heating
kúščar *n.m.* lizard
kuvérta *n.f.* envelope
kvadrát *n.m.* square; ~ **ni meter** *n.m.* square meter
kvalitéta *n.f.* quality
kvas *n.m.* yeast (*culin.*)

L

labód *n.m.* swan
laboratórij *n.m.* laboratory
láčen *adj.* hungry
ládja *n.f.* ship, boat, vessel
lagáti *v.* to lie
láhek *adj.* easy, light; **lahkomiseln** *adj.* thoughtless,
   reckless
lájati *v.* to bark, to bay
lak *n.m.* polish, varnish
lan *n.m.* flax; ~ **en pulover** *adj.* flaxen sweater
las *n.m.* hair; **dolgi ~je** *n.m.pl.* long hair
last *n.f.* property; **lásten** *adj.* own, proper

lastník *n.m.* owner, proprietor; **hišni** ~ *n.m.* landlord

lastnóst *n.f.* characteristic, feature

lástovica *n.f.* swallow (*zool.*)

lasúlja *n.f.* wig

latínica *n.f.* Latin alphabet

latínščina *n.f.* Latin

laž *n.f.* lie; **~en** *adj.* false

le *conj.* only, just, solely

léče *n.f.pl.* lenses; **kontaktne** ~ *n.f.pl.* contact lenses

led *n.m.* ice

ledén *adj.* ice, icy, glacial; **ledeni čaj** *n.m.* iced tea

ledeník *n.m.* glacier

ledvíca *n.f.* kidney; **vnetje ledvic** *n.nt.* nephritis

legálen *adj.* legal

lekárna *n.f.* pharmacy, drugstore

lékcija *n.f.* lesson, lecture

len *adj.* lazy, idle; **~ôba** *n.f.* laziness

lep *adj.* nice, handsome, pretty

lepílo *n.nt.* glue, paste

les *n.m.* wood; **~en** *adj.* wooden

léstev *n.f.* ladder; scale

léšnik *n.m.* hazelnut

let *n.m.* flight; ~ **alíšče** *n.nt.* airport; **~álo** *n.nt.* airplane, aircraft

letalska družba *n.f.* airline

letálski *adj.* air

letéti *v.* to fly; to run

létina *n.f.* crop, harvest

léto *n.nt.* year; **letos** *adv.* this year; **prihodnje** ~ *n.nt.* next year

letovíšče *n.nt.* (summer) resort

lêv *n.m.* lion

lév *adj.* left; **levíca** *n.f.* left hand

ležáti *v.* to lie, to be situated

líce *n.nt.* cheek

likálnik *n.m.* iron

líkati *v.* to iron

lílija *n.f.* lily
limóna *n.f.* lemon; **limonada** *n.f.* lemonade
lípa *n.f.* linden (tree)
lisíca *n.f.* fox
list *n.m.* leaf, sheet; **jedilni ~** *n.m.* menu
líter *n.m.* liter
literatúra *n.f.* literature
lízati *v.* to lick
lízika *n.f.* lollipop
ljub *adj.* dear, beloved
ljubézen *n.f.* love, affection; **ljubim te** I love you
ljubíti *v.* to love
ljubosúmnost *n.f.* jealousy
ljudjé *n.m.pl.* people
lóčen *adj.* separated; divorced
ločítev *n.f.* divorce; **ločenec** *n.m.* divorcé
lok *n.m.* bow, arch
lomíti *v.* to break
lônec *n.m.* pot; **cvetlični ~** *n.m.* flower pot
lopàr *n.m.* racket; **teniški ~** *n.m.* tennis racket
lopáta *n.f.* shovel, spade
lôpov *n.m.* thief, robber
lósos *n.m.* salmon
lovíti *n.* to chase, to hunt
lúbenica *n.f.* watermelon
luč *n.f.* light, lamp
lúka *n.f.* harbor, port
lúknja *n.f.* hole, gap
lúna *n.f.* moon; **polna ~** *n.f.* full moon

M

máčeha *n.f.* stepmother
máček *n.m.* cat; **mačka** *n.f.* female cat
mádež *n.m.* stain, spot
mah *n.m.* moss

maj *n.m.* May
májhen *adj.* little, small
májica *n.f.* T-shirt
majonéza *n.f.* mayonnaise
mak *n.m.* poppy
makaróni *n.m.pl.* macaroni
máksimalen *adj.* maximal, maximum
malénkost *n.f.* trifle, small matter
málica *n.f.* snack, refreshment
malína *n.f.* raspberry
málo *adv.* little, a little, few
mama, mati, mater *n.f.* mother; **mami** *n.f.* mommy
mamílo *n.nt.* drug, dope
mandarína *n.f.* mandarin
mándelj *n.m.* almond
manj *adv.* less
manjšína *n.f.* minority
mar *n.f.* care; **ni mi ~** I don't care
márati *v.* to like, to care for; **ne maram...** I don't like...
márec *n.m.* March
marélica *n.f.* apricot
margarína *n.f.* margarine
marmeláda *n.f.* jam, marmalade
mármor *n.m.* marble
masáža *n.f.* massage
máska *n.f.* mask
maslo *n.nt.* butter
mast *n.f.* fat, grease
máša *n.f.* mass
maščôba *n.f.* grease, fat
matemátika *n.f.* mathematics
materiál *n.m.* material; substance
materínščina *n.f.* mother tongue
matinéja *n.f.* matinee
matúra *n.f.* graduation (secondary school)
mávrica *n.f.* rainbow

mazílo *n.nt.* ointment
med *n.m.* honey; *prep.* among, during; **~eni tedni**
   n.m.pl. honeymoon
medálja *n.f.* medal
medicína *n.f.* medicine
mednároden *adj.* international; **mednarodna**
   trgovina *n.f.* international trade
medtém *prep.* while, during, in the meantime
mêdved *n.m.* bear
mêgla *n.f.* fog, mist
meháničen *adj.* mechanical
mehánik *n.m.* mechanic
mêhek *adj.* soft, tender
mehúr *n.m.* bladder
mêja *n.f.* border, frontier, boundary; limit
melodíja *n.f.* melody, tune
melóna *n.f.* melon
meníh *n.m.* monk
menjálnica *n.f.* exchange office
ménjati *v.* to change, to exchange
méra *n.f.* measure; extent
mériti *v.* to measure, to survey
mêsar *n.m.* butcher
mesec *n.m.* month; moon
mêso *n.nt.* meat, flesh; **~ na žaru** *n.nt.* grilled meat
mésto *n.* city, town; spot
méšati *v.* to mix, to stir
mêščan *n.m.* citizen
méta *n.f.* mint
meteorologija *n.f.* meteorology
méter *n.m.* meter; **kvadratni/kubični ~** *n.m.*
   square/cubic meter
mêtla *n.f.* broom
metúlj *n.m.* butterfly
mezínec *n.m.* pinky, little finger
mi *pron.* us, we
migréna *n.f.* migraine (headache)

milijón *n.m.* million

mílja *n.f.* mile; **morska ~** *n.f.* nautical mile

mílo *n.nt.* soap

mímo *prep.* by, past; **~grede** *adv.* by the way

minerál *n.m.* mineral; **~na voda** *n.f.* mineral water

mínimum *n.m.* minimum

miníster *n.m.* minister, secretary; **finančni ~** *n.m.* finance minister

minístrstvo *n.nt.* ministry

minúli *adj.* ago, past, gone; **~ teden** *n.m.* last week

minúta *n.f.* minute

mir *n.m.* peace, tranquility, quietness

míren *adj.* calm, peaceful, quiet, still

mísel *n.f.* thought, idea

mísliti *v.* to think, to meditate; **pre~** *v.* to rethink, think it over

miš *n.f.* mouse

míšica *n.f.* muscle

mit *n.m.* myth; **~ ologíja** *n.f.* mythology

míza *n.f.* table; **pisalna ~** *n.f.* writing desk; **~r** *n.f.* carpenter

mlad *adj.* young, youthful

mládič *n.m.* young one; puppy (*zool.*)

mladínski *adj.* juvenile, youth

mladoléten *adj.* minor, underage

mladóst *n.f.* youth, adolescence

mléko *n.nt.* milk

mlekárna *n.f.* dairy

mlin *n.m.* mill; **~ar** *n.m.* miller

mnênje *n.nt.* opinion, belief, view

mnógo *adv.* much, a great deal, many

mnóžica *n.f.* crowd, mass, multitude; **~ ljudi** *n.f.* crowd of people

množína *n.f.* plural; quantity

moč *n.f.* strength, power, force

môčen *adj.* strong, powerful

môči *v.* can, to be able; **ne morem ostati** I can't stay

močvírje *n.nt.* swamp, marsh

móda *n.f.* fashion, style

modél *n.m.* model, mold

móder *adj.* blue, azure; wise

modêren *adj.* modern, up-to-date

modrás *n.m.* viper

modróst *n.f.* wisdom; **~ ni zob** *n.m.* wisdom tooth

mogóče *adv.* maybe, perhaps

moj *pron.* my; mine

mójster *n.m.* master, skilled laborer

móka *n.f.* flour

móker *adj.* wet, soaked

molítev *n.f.* prayer

molíti *v.* to pray

môlj *n.m.* moth

monárh *n.m.* monarch; **~íja** *n.f.* monarchy

morála *n.f.* morality

mórati *v.* must, have to

mordà *adv.* perhaps, maybe (also **mogoče**)

moríti *v.* to murder, to kill

mórje *n.nt.* sea, ocean; **odprto ~** *n.nt.* open sea

mornár *n.m.* sailor; seaman

most *n.m.* bridge

mošéja *n.f.* mosquc (*relig.*)

môški *n.m.* male, man; **samski ~** *n.m.* bachelor

mótiti *v.* to bother, to disturb

motív *n.m.* motive

motòr *n.m.* engine; motorbike

mozaík *n.m.* mosaic

móž *n.m.* man; husband; **bivši ~** *n.m.* ex-husband

možgáni *n.m.pl.* brain(s)

móžnost *n.f.* possibility, chance, opportunity

mrak *n.m.* dusk

mrávlja *n.f.* ant; **mravljišče** *n.nt.* anthill

mraz *n.m.* cold, chill, frost

mréža *n.f.* net

mrk *n.m.* eclipse; **sončni** ~ *n.m.* solar eclipse
mŕtev *adj.* dead, lifeless
mŕzel *adj.* cold, chilly, icy
mŕzlica *n.f.* fever
múha *n.f.* fly
mulát *n.m.* mulatto
muslimán *n.m.* Moslem/Muslim
muzéj *n.m.* museum
múzika *n.f.* music

N

na *prep.* on, upon, in; to; ~ **cesti** *prep.* on the street;
~ **zdravje!** *interj.* cheers!
nacionálen *adj.* national
načín *n.m.* way, manner, mode; **na isti** ~ *adv.* in the
same way
načŕt *n.m.* plan, project; design; **potovalni** ~ *n.m.*
itinerary
nad *prep.* above, over; ~ **nami** *prep.* above us
nadev *n.m.* stuffing (*culin.*)
nadomésten *adj.* spare; ~ **del** *n.m.* spare part
nadstrópje *n.nt.* floor, story; **v tretjem nadstropju**
prep. on the third floor
nadzôr *n.m.* control; ~**nik** *n.m.* supervisor, controller
naênkrat *adv.* suddenly
nag *adj.* naked, nude
nagón *n.m.* instinct
nagráda *n.f.* prize, award
nahŕbtnik *n.m.* backpack, knapsack
najbólje *adv.* the best
najbóljši *adj.* the best
najbrž *adv.* probably, likely
najemnína *n.f.* rent; **mesečna** ~ *n.f.* monthly rent
najéti *v.* to rent, to hire
nájmanj *adv.* the least

nájmanjši *adj.* smallest
nájstnik *n.m.* teenager
nájti *v.* to find, to discover
nájveč *adv.* the most
nájvečji *adj.* the biggest
nakít *n.m.* jewelry
nakúp *n.m.* purchase
nalépka *n.f.* sticker, label
nalezljív *adj.* contagious
nalóga *n.f.* task, exercise; **domača** ~ *n.f.* homework
namèn *n.m.* aim, intention, purpose
namésto *adv.* instead of, in place of
namíg *n.m.* hint
napáčen *adj.* wrong, false
napáka *n.f.* mistake, fault, defect, failure
napétost *n.f.* tension; strain; **visoka/nizka** ~ *n.f.* high/low tension
napíhniti *v.* to blow up, to puff up
napísati *v.* to write (down)
napitnína *n.f.* tip; **dati napitníno** *v.* to tip
napólniti *v.* to fill (up)
napóved *n.f.* announcement, forecast; **vremenska** ~ *n.f.* weather forecast
napráva *n.f.* device, machine
napréj *adv.* forward, ahead, on, onwards
napródaj *interj.* for sale
narámnice *n.f.pl.* straps
naráva *n.f.* nature; **naravno bogastvo** *n.nt.* natural sources
narávnost *adv.* straight
naréčje *n.nt.* dialect
naredíti *v.* to make, to do
narkóza *n.f.* narcosis
naróbe *adv.* wrong
naročíti *v.* to order; to subscribe
naročnína *n.f.* subscription
národ *n.m.* nation, people

národen *adj.* national; **narodni praznik** *n.m.*
national holiday

národnost *n.f.* nationality

naslédnji *adj.* next, following

naslòv *n.m.* address; title; **~na stran** *n.f.* front page

nasméh *n.m.* smile

naspróten *adj.* contrary, opposite

naspróti *adv.* opposite (to), in front of

nastanítev *n.f.* accommodation, lodging

nastòp *n.m.* conduct, performance

nasvèt *n.m.* advice, suggestion; **prositi za ~** *v.* to
ask for advice

naš *pron.* our, ours

natakar *n.m.* waiter; **~ica** *n.f.* waitress

natánčen *adj.* exact, accurate, precise

natò *adv.* then, after, afterwards; **NATO** *n.m.* NATO

naváda *n.f.* custom, habit

naváden *adj.* ordinary, regular, usual; **ne~** *adj.*
unusual, extraordinary

navodílo *n.nt.* instruction, direction

nazáj *adv.* back; backwards; **vzeti ~** *v.* to take back

ne *adv.* no, not

nebó *n.nt.* sky; **~ tičnik** *n.m.* skyscraper

nečák *n.m.* nephew

nečákinja *n.f.* niece

nedélja *n.f.* Sunday

néga *n.f.* care, treatment

néhati *v.* to stop, to quit

nékaj *adv.* something, any, few; **imam ~ zate** I
have something for you

nekdánji *adj.* ex, former

nékdo *pron.* somebody, someone

nemogóč *adj.* impossible

nenádoma *adv.* suddenly

neodvísen *adj.* independent

nepáren *adj.* odd; **neparno število** *n.nt.* odd number

nepravílen *adj.* incorrect, wrong

nepremičnína *n.f.* estate; **nepremičninska agencija** *n.f.* real estate agency

nervózen *adj.* nervous

nesporazúm *n.m.* misunderstanding, misapprehension

nesrámen *adj.* unkind, rude, impolite

nesréča *n.f.* accident; **prometna ~** *n.f.* car accident

netopír *n.m.* bat

neudóben *adj.* uncomfortable

neúmen *adj.* stupid, foolish, silly

neúrje *n.nt.* thunderstorm

neváren *adj.* dangerous, unsafe

neveljáven *adj.* invalid

nevésta *n.f.* bride

nevíhta *n.f.* tempest, storm

nezaposlèn *adj.* unemployed

nezavésten *adj.* unconscious

neznán *adj.* unknown, strange; **~ec** *n.m.* stranger

nič *n.* zero

ničla (nula) *n.* nothing; zero

nihčè *pron.* nobody, no one

níkdar, nikoli *adv.* never

nízek *adj.* low, shallow

njegóv *adj.* his

njen *adj.* her

njíhov *adj.* their

njíva *n.f.* field

njun *adj.* their (*du.*)

nocój *adv.* tonight

noč *n.f.* night

nôga *n.f.* leg, foot; **~více** *n.f.pl.* socks

nogomèt *n.m* soccer; **~áš** *n.m.* soccer player

noht *n.m.* nail

nor *adj.* mad, crazy; **~ost** *n.f.* madness, lunacy

noríce *n.f.pl.* chickenpox

normálen *adj.* normal, ordinary

nos *n.m.* nose

noséčnost *n.f.* pregnancy

nosíti *v.* to carry, to bear; to wear (clothes)

nóša *n.f.* costume, dress; **narodna** ~ *n.f.* national garb

notár *n.m.* notary

nótranji *adj.* inner, internal, interior; **notranjost** *n.f.* inland, interior

nov *adj.* new, recent

novémber *n.m.* November

novíca *n.f.* a piece of news, news

novínar *n.m.* journalist

nož *n.m.* knife

nújen *adj.* urgent

O

o *prep.* about; ~ **čem se pogovarjate?** what are you talking about?

ob *prep.* at, along, on; ~ **vodi** *prep.* along the river; ~ **treh** *prep.* at three o'clock

oba *n.* both

obála *n.f.* coast, shore; **obalna straža** *n.f.* coast guard

óbčina *n.f.* municipality

občínstvo *n.nt.* audience

občútek *n.* feeling, sensation; **slab/dober** ~ *n.m.* bad/good feeling

občutljív *adj.* delicate, sensitive

obésiti *v.* to hang

obešálnik *n.m.* (coat) hanger

običáj *n.m.* custom, tradition

obísk *n.m.* visit; ~**áti** *v.* to visit, to attend; ~**oválec** *n.m.* visitor

oblák *n.m.* cloud; **oblačno vreme** *n.nt.* cloudy weather

obléči *v.* to put on, to dress

obléka *n.f.* clothing, clothes

oblétnica *n.f.* anniversary
oblíka *n.f.* form, shape
oblíž *n.m.* patch, plaster
obljuba *n.f.* promise; **obljubíti** *v.* to promise
obmóčje *n.nt.* area, region
obnovíti *v.* to renew
oboževálec *n.m.* fan
obráz *n.m.* face
obrázec *n.m.* form; **izpolniti ~** *v.* to fill out a form
obrésti *n.f.pl.* interest rate
obríti *v.* to shave
obŕt *n.f.* craft, handicraft
obŕv *n.f.* eyebrow
obútev *n.f.* footwear
obúti *v.* to put on shoes
obvestílo *n.nt.* communication, notification
obvéza *n.f.* bandage
obvézen *adj.* obligatory, mandatory
oceán *n.m.* ocean, sea; **Tihi ~** *n.m.* Pacific Ocean
océna *n.f.* mark, critique; estimate
ocvrt *adj.* fried; **~ piščanec** *n.m.* fried chicken
očála *n.f.pl.* eyeglasses
ôče *n.m.* father; **oči, očka** *n.* daddy; **očim** *n.m.*
    stepfather
od *prep.* of, from
odbijáč *n.m.* bumper (*autom.*)
odbójka *n.f.* volleyball
oddáljen *adj.* distant, remote
oddati *v.* to let, to lease; to deliver
oddélek *n.m.* department, division
odéja *n.f.* blanket
óder *n.m.* stage, platform
odgóvor *n.m.* answer, reply; **~íti** *v.* to answer, to reply
odgovórnost *n.f.* responsibility
odhód *n.m.* departure
odíti *v.* to leave, to part
odkleníti *v.* unlock

odlíčen *adj.* excellent, fine
odločíti se *v.* to decide
odpiráč *n.m.* can opener
odpréti *v.* to open; **odprto od... do...** open from... to...
odpôved *n.f.* cancellation, abolition; **odpovédati** *v.* to cancel
odrásel *adj.* grown-up, adult
odstótek *n.m.* percentage
odvétnik *n.m.* lawyer; **odvetniška pisarna** *n.f.* law office
odvijáč *n.m.* screwdriver
odvísen *adj.* dependent; **biti ~ od** *v.* to depend on
ôgenj *n.m.* fire
oglás *n.m.* advertisement, announcement
ogledálo *n.nt.* mirror
óglje *n.nt.* charcoal
ognjíšče *n.nt.* fireplace
ográja *n.f.* fence, barrier
ogréti *v.* to warm, to heat
ogrômen *adj.* enormous, huge
ôkno *n.nt.* window
ôkó *n.nt.* eye
okólica *n.f.* surroundings
okrás *n.m.* decoration, ornament
okrepčeválnica *n.f.* snack bar
okrógel *adj.* round, circular
október *n.m.* October
okús *n.m.* taste, flavor; **~iti** *v.* to taste
okúžba *n.f.* infection
okvír *n.m.* frame
olimpijáda *n.f.* Olympic Games
olíva *n.f.* olive; olive tree; **olivno olje** *n.nt.* olive oil
olje *n.nt.* oil; **ricinusovo ~** *n.nt.* castor oil
omáka *n.f.* sauce, gravy, dressing
omára *n.f.* closet
omedléti *v.* to faint

on *pron.m.* he
ona *pron.f.* her
onadva *pron.dual* they
oni *pron.pl.* they
ono *pron.nt.* it
ópera *n.f.* opera
operácija *n.f.* operation; surgery
ópica *n.f.* monkey, ape
opisáti *v.* to describe
opóldne *adv.* midday
opólnoči *adv.* midnight
oporóka *n.f.* will, testament
opozorílo *n.nt.* warning, notice, caution
opravičilo *n.nt.* excuse
opravíčiti se *v.* to apologize
opréma *n.f.* equipment, outfit
oprostíti *v.* to forgive, to pardon; **oprostite!** *interj.*
  excuse me!
óptik *n.m.* optician
oránžen *adj.* orange (*col.*)
ôreh *n.m.* walnut; walnut tree
organizácija *n.f.* organization
originál *n.m.* original
orkéster *n.m.* orchestra, band
oródje *n.nt.* tools, instruments
oróžje *n.nt.* arms, weapon
ôsa *n.f.* wasp
oséba *n.f.* person
osében *adj.* personal; **osebna izkaznica** *n.f.*
  personal identification card
osébje *n.nt.* staff
ôsel *n.m.* donkey
ósem *num.* eight
osnóven *adj.* elementary, basic; **osnovna šola** *n.f.*
  elementary school
ostáti *v.* to stay, to remain
óster *adj.* sharp, pointed

ostríga *n.f.* oyster
oteklína *n.f.* inflammation
ôtok *n.m.* island, isle
otròk *n.m.* child; **otroci** *n.m.pl.* children
otróštvo *n.nt.* childhood
ôvca *n.f.* sheep
ovčár *n.m.* shepherd; **nemški** ~ *n.m.* German shepherd
ovínek *n.m.* turn, corner
ovrátnik *n.m.* collar
ozek *adj.* narrow, tight
ozémlje *n.nt.* territory

P

pa *conj.* but, however; end
paciént *n.m.* patient
pájek *n.m.* spider
pakét *n.m.* parcel, packet
pakírati *v.* to pack; **raz~** *v.* to unpack
paláča *n.f.* palace, mansion
palačínka *n.f.* pancake, crêpe
pálec *n.m.* thumb; inch (2.54 cm)
pálica *n.f.* stick, pole
palúba *n.f.* deck
pámeten *adj.* clever, intelligent
pápir *n.m.* paper
páprika *n.f.* pepper; **zelena** ~ *n.f.* green pepper
par *n.m.* pair, couple
paradížnik *n.m.* tomato
parfúm *n.m.* perfume, fragrance
park *n.m.* park
parkírati *v.* to park
parkiríšče *n.nt.* parking lot
parlamènt *n.m.* parliament
pártner *n.m.* partner
pas *n.m.* waist; belt

pásti *v.* to fall, to drop

pastorek *n.m.* stepson; **pastorka** *n.f.* stepdaughter

paštéta *n.f.* pâté

páziti (na) *v.* to take care (of), to pay attention to

peč *n.f.* stove, oven; **~enka** *n.f.* roast beef **pêči** *v.* to bake; **pečíca** *n.f.* oven

pek *n.m.* baker; **~arna** *n.f.* bakery

peljáti *v.* to lead, to guide; to drive

pénzija *n.f.* pension

pepél *n.m.* ash; **~nik** *n.m.* ashtray

perílo *n.nt.* clothes; **spodnje ~** *n.nt.* underwear

perón *n.m.* platform

pes *n.m.* dog; **morski ~** *n.m.* shark

pések *n.m.* sand

pésem *n.f.* song, melody, poem

pésnik *n.m.* poet

péšec *n.m.* pedestrian; **prehod za pešče** *n.m.* crosswalk

pet *num.* five

pêta *n.f.* heel; **visoke pete** *n.f.pl.* high heels

pétek *n.m.* Friday

peteršílj *n.m.* parsley

péti *v.* to sing

pévec *n.m.* singer; **pevka** *n.f.* singer

píhati *v.* to blow, to puff

pijáča *n.f.* beverage, drink

piján *adj.* drunk

píknik *n.m.* picnic

pisárna *n.f.* office

pisáti *v.* to write, to take note

písmo *n.nt.* letter (post); **priporočeno ~** *n.m.* registered letter

piščánec *n.m.* chicken

piškót *n.m.* cookie

pištóla *n.f.* gun

píti *v.* to drink

pívo *n.nt.* beer; **~varna** *n.f.* brewery

pižáma *n.f.* pajamas

pláča *n.f.* salary, income, wage

pláčati *v.* to pay

planína *n.f.* mountain

plástika *n.f.* plastic

plašč *n.m.* coat

plaválec *n.m.* swimmer

plávati *v.* to swim

pláz *n.m.* avalanche

pleníce *n.f.pl.* diaper

ples *n.m.* dance; **~áti** *v.* to dance

plesálec *n.m.* male dancer

plesálka *n.f.* female dancer

pléšast *adj.* bald

plézati *v.* to climb

plin *n.m.* gas

pljúča *n.f.pl.* lungs; **pljučnica** *n.f.* pneumonia

plóčnik *n.m.* pavement

plôšča *n.f.* record, LP

plóvba *n.f.* navigation (*mar.*)

po *adv.* after, on, upon, through

pocéni *adj.* cheap, inexpensive; **pre~** *adj.* too cheap

počásen *adj.* slow

počítnice *n.f.pl.* holiday, vacation

počívati *v.* to rest

pod *adv.* under, below; *n.m.* floor

podáljšek *n.m.* extension

podhód *n.m.* subway pass

podjétje *n.nt.* company, firm

podnébje *n.nt.* climate; **mediteransko ~** *n.m.*
   Mediterranean climate

podóben *adj.* alike, similar, resembling

podpís *n.m.* signature, autograph; **~ati** *v.* to sign

podróčje *n.nt.* area, section

podstréšje *n.nt.* attic, loft

poglávje *n.nt.* chapter

pogôj *n.m.* condition, circumstance

pogóltniti *v.* to swallow
pogósto *adv.* often, frequently
pogóvor *n.m.* conversation, chat
pogréb *n.m.* funeral
pogréšati *v.* to miss, to lack
pohíštvo *n.nt.* furniture
pohitéti *v.* to hurry up
poiskáti *v.* to seek, to look for
poizkúsiti *v.* to try, to attempt
poizvedováti *v.* to inquire, to investigate
pojédina *n.f.* feast
pokázati *v.* to show; to point at; to display
poklíc *n.m.* profession, occupation
pokojnína *n.f.* pension
pokopalíšče *n.nt.* cemetery
pokrájina *n.f.* landscape
pokríti *v.* to cover
pokrôv *n.m.* cover
pokvárjen *adj.* rotten (*culin.*); broken
pol *n.m.* half; pole; ~ **ure** *n.f.* half an hour; **Severni**
~ *n.m.* North Pole
polétje *n.nt.* summer
políca *n.f.* shelf
policíja *n.f.* police; **policist** *n.m.* policeman
polítika *n.f.* politics; policy
pólje *n.nt.* field
poljúbiti *v.* to kiss
pólniti *v.* to fill, to charge; **na~** *v.* to refill
pôlnjen *adj.* stuffed, filled
polnóč *n.f.* midnight
pôlog *n.m.* deposit
polôtok *n.m.* peninsula
pôlž *n.m.* snail
pomágati *v.* to help, to aid
pomaránča *n.f.* orange
pomémben *adj.* important, significant
pomên *n.m.* meaning

pomívati *v.* to wash up
pomlád *n.f.* spring
pomóč *n.f.* aid, help; **prva ~** *n.f.* first aid
pomôl *n.m.* pier
pomóta *n.f.* mistake, error
ponedéljek *n.m.* Monday
pônev *n.f.* saucepan
ponovíti *v.* to repeat
ponôvno *adv.* again, once more
ponúdba *n.f.* offer, proposal
pópek *n.m.* bellybutton
pôper *n.m.* pepper
popôldne *n.nt.* afternoon (P.M.)
popóln *adj.* perfect, complete
popráviti *v.* to fix, to repair
populáren *adj.* popular, fashionable
por *n.m.* leek
porábiti *v.* to spend, to waste
pórcija *n.f.* portion
poročén *adj.* married
poróka *n.f.* wedding; marriage
posében *adj.* special
pôsel *n.m.* business, affair, work; deal
posést *n.f.* property, possession; estate
poskús *n.m.* experiment; **~iti** *v.* to try
posladek *n.m.* dessert (*culin.*)
posláti *v.* to send, to mail
poslúšati *v.* to listen
posodíti *v.* to lend
postaja(líšče) *n.f.* station
postáti *v.* to become
postáviti *v.* to put, to set
póstelja *n.f.* bed
postréžba *n.f.* service; **samo~** *n.f.* self-service
postŕv *n.f.* trout; **Soška ~** *n.f.* Soča trout
poškódba *n.f.* injury, lesion

pôšten *adj.* honest, sincere; **~ost** *n.f.* honesty, integrity

póšta *n.f.* post, post office; **poštni nabiralnik** *n.m.* post office box

pót *n.f.* way, path

pôt *n.m.* sweat

potapljáč *n.m.* (scuba) diver

pôtem *adv.* after, afterwards

potísniti *v.* to push

pótnik *n.m.* passenger, traveler

potovánje *n.nt.* trip, journey

potováti *v.* to travel, to tour

potrdílo *n.nt.* certificate, confirmation

potrdíti *v.* to confirm

potrébno *adj.* necessary, urgent

potrebováti *v.* to need

potróšnik *n.m.* consumer

poučeváti *v.* to teach

povabílo *n.nt.* invitation

povábiti *v.* to invite

povéčati *v.* to increase, to maximize

povédati *v.* to tell, to let know

povézati *v.* to connect; **slaba povezava** *n.f.* bad connection

povléči *v.* to pull

povpréčen *adj.* average, mediocre

površína *n.f.* surface

povsód *adv.* everywhere

pozabíti *v.* to forget

pozdráviti *v.* to greet, to welcome; **lep pozdrav!** *interj.* kind regards!

pôzen *adj.* late

pozôr! *interj.* attention! caution!

pozórnost *n.f.* attention, consideration

požár *n.m.* fire

Praga *n.f.* Prague

prah *n.m.* dust

prálnica *n.f.* laundry

práti *v.* to wash

prav *interj.* okay, all right, fine

právi *adj.* real, proper; correct

pravíca *n.f.* justice

pravílo *n.nt.* rule, principle; **po pravilih** *adv.* by the rules

právo *n.nt.* law

prázen *adj.* empty, vacant

práznik *n.m.* holiday

praznováti *v.* to celebrate

prebáva *n.f.* digestion; **slaba ~** *n.f.* indigestion

prebiválci *n.m.pl.* inhabitants, population

pred *adv.* before, in front, ahead

predál *n.m.* drawer

predméstje *n.nt.* suburb

prêdmet *n.m.* thing, item, object

prédnost *n.f.* advantage

predsédnik *n.m.* president; chairman (*bus.*)

predstáva *n.f.* show, performance; idea, notion

predstáviti *v.* to introduce, to present

preglêd *n.m.* examination, revision

prehlád *n.m.* cold, chill

prekíniti *v.* to interrupt

prekôp *n.m.* channel

premákniti *v.* to move

prêmog *n.m.* coal

prenočíšče *n.nt.* hostel; **mladinsko ~** *n.nt.* youth hostel

preoblačílnica *n.f.* changing room

prepád *n.m.* abyss

prepírati se *v.* to argue

prepovédati *v.* to forbid, to prohibit

prepoznáti *v.* to recognize

prepróga *n.f.* rug, carpet

prepróst *adj.* easy, simple

presenéčenje *n.nt.* surprise

prestáva *n.f.* gear, transmission (*autom.*)

prevajálec *n.m.* translator
prevèč *adv.* too much, too many
prevériti *v.* to check, to verify
prevêsti *v.* to translate
prevíden *adj.* careful; **bodi ~** be careful
prevôd *n.m.* translation
prevôz *n.m.* transport; **~nik** *n.m.* carrier, transporter
prha *n.f.* shower
pri *prep.* at, by, near
približno *adv.* about, approximately
pribôr *n.m.* cutlery
príča *n.f.* witness
pričakováti *v.* to expect
pričéska *n.f.* hairdo, hairstyle
pridévnik *n.m.* adjective
pridrúžiti se *v.* to join
prigrízek *n.m.* snack
prihódnost *n.f.* future
priimek *n.m.* surname, last name
prijátelj *n.m.* friend; **prijateljica** *n.f.* friend
prijáviti (se) *v.* to check in; to declare
prijázen *adj.* kind, polite
prijéten *adj.* nice, pleasant; **ne~** *adj.* unpleasant
prikólica *n.f.* trailer
prilépiti *v.* to paste (on), to stick (on)
prilóžnost *n.f.* occasion, opportunity, chance
primér *n.m.* case, example; **na ~** for example
prinêsti *v.* to bring
pripéti *v.* to fasten; **~ varnostni pas** *v.* to fasten
  one's seat belt
pripomóček *n.m.* accessory
pripráviti *v.* to prepare
pristaníšče *n.nt.* harbor, port
príti *v.* to come, to arrive
pritôžba *n.f.* complaint
privóščiti si *v.* to afford
prižgáti *v.* to set on fire

problém *n.m.* problem
prodája *n.f.* sale; **prodajalec-ka** *n.m.*, *n.f.*
    salesperson, clerk
prodajálna *n.f.* shop
prodáti *v.* to sell
profésor *n.m.* professor
proizvódnja *n.f.* production, fabrication
promèt *n.m.* traffic, circulation
prósim *interj.* please
prost *adj.* free, vacant
próti *adv.* against; towards; **~zmrzovalno sredstvo**
    n.nt. antifreeze
pŕsi *n.f.pl.* chest; breast
prst *n.m.* finger; **~an** *n.m.* ring
prt *n.m.* tablecloth
prtíček *n.m.* napkin
prtljága *n.f.* luggage, baggage; **prtljážnik** *n.m.*
    trunk
prvák *n.m.* champion
pŕvi *num.* first; **prvorazreden** *adj.* first-class,
    first-rate
psihiáter *n.m.* psychiatric, shrink
pšeníca *n.f.* wheat
ptíca *n.f.* bird
púding *n.m.* pudding
pulôver *n.m.* jumper, pullover, sweater; cardigan
pustíti *v.* to let, to permit
pustolóvščina *n.f.* adventure
puščáva *n.f.* desert
púščica *n.f.* arrow

R

rábiti *v.* to use, to employ
ráca *n.f.* duck

račún *n.m.* bill, check, receipt; account, invoice; **tekočì** ~ *n.* checking account

računálnik *n.m.* computer; **računalniški program** *n.m.* computer program

računáti *v.* to count

rádio *n.m.* radio

radovéden *adj.* curious

rákovica *n.f.* crab

ráma *n.f.* shoulder

rána *n.f.* injury, lesion, wound; **biti ranjen** *v.* to be hurt

ránjenec *n.m.* casualty, wounded person

rása *n.f.* race

rásti *v.* to grow; **od~** *v.* to grow up

rastlína *n.f.* plant, vegetable

ráven *adj.* plane, flat

razdálja *n.f.* distance

razdelíti *v.* divide, split

rázen *conj.* except, apart from

razglèd *n.m.* view, outlook

razglédnica *n.f.* postcard; ~ **z znamkami** *n.f.* postcard with stamps

raziskáva *n.f.* investigation, research

razkóšen *adj.* luxurious

razlíčica *n.f.* version; **najnovejša** ~ *n.f.* the latest version

razlíka *n.f.* difference

rázlog *n.m.* reason, motive

razložiti *v.* to explain

razmérje *n.nt.* relation(ship)

razpoložljív *adv.* available

razprávljati *v.* to discuss

razprodája *n.f.* sales

rázred *n.m.* class, category; **prvi** ~ *n.m.* first class

razstáva *n.f.* exhibition

razšíriti *v.* to expand

razúm *n.m.* intellect, mind, reason

razuméti *v.* to understand, to comprehend; **ne razumem** I don't understand

razvedrílo *n.nt.* entertainment, amusement

rdeč *adj.* red; **~elás** *adj.* red-haired

rêbrce *n.nt.* rib (*culin.*)

recépcija *n.f.* reception

recépt *n.m.* prescription; cooking recipe

rêči *v.* to say, to tell

rédek *adj.* rare, unusual

rêdkev *n.f.* radish

rédko *adv.* rarely, seldom

rédno *adv.* regularly, frequently

régija *n.f.* region

réka *n.f.* river

rekláma *n.f.* advertisement, commercial

rekórd *n.m.* record; **svetovni ~** *n.m.* world record

rekreácija *n.f.* recreation

renesánsa *n.f.* renaissance

réntgen *n.m.* X ray

rep *n.m.* tail (*zool.*)

repúblika *n.f.* republic

res *adv.* really; **ali ~?** really?

résen *adj.* serious, grave

resníca *n.f.* truth

resníčen *adj.* real, true

restavrácija *n.f.* restaurant; **samopostrežna ~** *n.f.* cafeteria, self-service

réšiti *v.* to rescue, to save; **rešilni avto** *n.m.* ambulance

réven *adj.* poor

revíja *n.f.* magazine; **~ o modi** *n.f.* fashion magazine

révščina *n.f.* poverty

rézati *v.* to cut, to slice; **od~** *v.* to cut off

rezervácija *n.f.* reservation

rezervírati *v.* to make a reservation

rezultát *n.m.* result; score (*sp.*)

ríba *n.f.* fish; **~riti** *v.* to fish
ríbič *n.m.* fisherman
Rim *n.m.* Rome
rísanka *n.f.* cartoon
rísati *v.* to draw, to paint
riž *n.m.* rice
rjav *adj.* brown
rjúha *n.f.* sheet
róbček *n.m.* tissue; **papirnati ~** *n.m.* tissue paper
robídnica *n.f.* blackberry
rôjen *adj.* born; **rojstni dan** *n.m.* birthday
rôka *n.f.* hand; arm; **rokavica** *n.f.* glove; **rokáv**
 n.m. sleeve
romántičen *adj.* romantic
rozína *n.f.* currant, raisin
róža *n.f.* flower
rum *n.m.* rum
rumèn *adj.* yellow (*col.*)

S

s/z *prep.* with, along with, in the company of; from
sádje *n.nt.* fruit
saksofón *n.m.* saxophone
saláma *n.f.* salami
sam *adj.* alone
samó *adv.* only, solely
samodéjen *adj.* automatic
samostálnik *n.m.* noun (*gram.*)
samostán *n.m.* monastery, convent
sámski *adj.* single
saní *n.f.pl.* sled
sánjati *v.* to dream
sánje *n.f.pl.* dreams
sardíne *n.f.pl.* sardines

sebíčnež *n.m.* egoist
sedáj *adv.* now, at present
sédem *num.* seven
sedéti *v.* to sit
sédež *n.m.* seat; ~**nica** *n.f.* chairlift
sêjem *n.m.* fair; market; **bolšji** ~ *n.m.* flea market
sekíra *n.f.* hatchet
sekúnda *n.f.* second
sem *adv.* here; **pridi** ~ come (over) here
semafór *n.m.* traffic light, semaphore
sénca *n.f.* shade, shadow
séndvič *n.m.* sandwich
septêmber *n.m.* September
servírati *v.* to serve
sêrvis *n.m.* service, repair; **avto~** *n.m.* car repair
  (*autom.*)
sesálnik *n.m.* vacuum cleaner
sestánek *n.m.* appointment, meeting
sêstra *n.f.* sister; **sestrična** *n.f.* female cousin;
  medicinska ~ *n.f.* nurse
sevéda *adv.* of course, certainly
séver *n.m.* north; **severni** *adj.* northern
sêznam *n.m.* list, register
sezóna *n.f.* season; **visoka/nizka** ~ *n.f.* high/low
  season
sídro *n.nt.* anchor (*mar.*)
sijáj *n.m.* shine
síla *n.f.* emergency, force, need
simból *n.m.* symbol
simptóm *n.m.* symptom
sin *n.m.* son; **najstarejši** ~ *n.m.* the oldest son
sir *n.m.* cheese
sírup *n.m.* syrup
sistém *n.m.* system
situácija *n.f.* situation
siv *adj.* gray

skála *n.f.* rock, cliff
skávt *n.m.* scout
skiró *n.nt.* scooter
skladíšče *n.nt.* warehouse
skočíti *v.* to jump
skodélica *n.f.* cup
skôraj *adv.* almost, nearly
skózi *prep.* through, throughout
skrb *n.f.* care, worry; **~éti** *v.* to take care, to worry
skríti *v.* to hide
skrivnóst *n.f.* secret
skrômen *adj.* modest
skúpaj *adv.* together, jointly
skupína *n.f.* group
slab *adj.* bad; **slabó** *adv.* badly, poorly
sládkor *n.m.* sugar; **~na bolezen** *n.f.* diabetes
sládek *adj.* sweet
sladoléd *n.m.* ice cream
slan *adj.* salty; **~a** *n.f.* frost
slanína *n.f.* bacon
slap *n.m.* cascade, waterfall
slaščičárna *n.f.* pastry shop, confectionery
sláven *adj.* famous, celebrated
sledíti *v.* to follow
slíka *n.f.* picture, painting; **~r** *n.m.* painter
slíkati *v.* to paint; to take a photo
slíšati *v.* to listen
slíva *n.f.* plum
slôj *n.m.* layer
slon *n.m.* elephant
slovár *n.m.* dictionary; **žepni ~** *n.m.* pocket dictionary
slóvnica *n.f.* grammar
slúžba *n.f.* job, work, employment
smejáti se *v.* to laugh
smer *n.f.* direction, course
smétana *n.f.* cream; **stepena ~** *n.f.* whipped cream

smêti *n.m.pl.* garbage, rubbish

smrdéti *v.* to stink

smrt *n.f.* death

smúčati *v.* to ski

snáha *n.f.* daughter-in-law

sneg *n.m.* snow

snežíti *v.* to snow

sôba *n.f.* room, chamber; **dnevna** ~ *n.f.* living room

sobóta *n.f.* Saturday

sodelovánje *n.nt.* collaboration, cooperation

sodíšče *n.nt.* court

sodnìk-ca *n.m.* judge, arbitrator

sok *n.m.* juice

sol *n.f.* salt

soláta *n.f.* salad; lettuce; **paradižnikova** ~ *n.f.* tomato salad

solíti *v.* to salt, to add salt

sôlze *n.f.pl.* tears

sónce *n.nt.* sun

sónčiti se *v.* to sunbathe

sónčnik *n.m.* sunshade

soródstvo *n.nt.* relatives

sósed *n.m.* neighbor

sovrážiti *v.* to hate, to detest

spálnica *n.f.* bedroom

spáti *v.* to sleep; to nap

specialitéta *n.f.* specialty; **hišna** ~ *n.f.* house specialty (*culin.*)

splôšen *adj.* general

spôdaj *adv.* down, downstairs

spol *n.m.* sex, gender

spomeník *n.m.* monument, statue

spomín *n.m.* memory; **~ek** *n.m.* souvenir

spômniti se *v.* to remember

sporočílo *n.nt.* message, note; **novo** ~ *n.m.* new message

sposóbnost *n.f.* skill, capacity

spoznáti *v.* to meet, to get to know

sprêhod *n.m.* walk, stroll; **iti na ~** *v.* to take a walk

sprejéti *v.* to receive, to accept

spremémba *n.f.* change

sprémljati *v.* to accompany

sprétnost *n.f.* skill, ability; **ročna ~** *n.f.* manual skills

sprevódnik *n.m.* conductor

sprostíti se *v.* to relax

srájca *n.f.* shirt

sramežljív *adj.* shy

sramôta *n.f.* shame

srce *n.nt.* heart; **srčni utrip** *n.m.* heartbeat

srebró *n.nt.* silver; **srebŕen** *adj.* silver (*col.*)

sréča *n.f.* happiness, luck, chance, fortune

sréčati *v.* to meet

sréda *n.f.* Wednesday

sredína *n.f.* middle, midst, center

sredíšče *n.nt.* center; **~ mesta** *n.nt.* city center

srednjevéški *adj.* medieval

srédnji *adj.* middle; **srednja velikost** *n.f.* medium size

sredozémlje *n.nt.* Mediterranean

stádion *n.m.* stadium

stánje *n.nt.* condition, state, situation

stanovánje *n.nt.* flat, apartment

stanováti *v.* to live, to reside; **stanujem v Celju** I live in Celje

star *adj.* old, aged; **~inski** *adj.* ancient

stárši *n.m.pl.* parents; **stari ~** *n.m.pl.* grandparents

státi *v.* to stand; to cost

stávek *n.m.* sentence

stêber *n.m.* column

stêklo *n.nt.* glass

stevardésa *n.f.* flight attendant

stik *n.m.* connection, contact

stikálo *n.nt.* switch
sto *num.* hundred
stôl *n.m.* chair
stolétje *n.nt.* century
stolp *n.m.* tower
stopálo *n.nt.* foot
stopínja *n.f.* degree (temperature)
stôpnice *n.f.pl.* stairs; **tekoče** ~ *n.f.pl.* escalator
stôpnja *n.f.* level, stage, degree
storítev *n.f.* service
strah *n.m.* fear, terror
stran *n.f.* side; page; **pojdi ~!** go away!
straníšče *n.nt.* toilet, WC
stránka *n.f.* client, customer
strášen *adj.* awful, terrible, horrible
straža *n.f.* guard
stréha *n.f.* roof
stríc *n.m.* uncle
strínjati se *v.* to agree
strôj *n.m.* machine, device
strôp *n.m.* ceiling
stróšek *n.m.* expense, cost
strúna *n.f.* string; **kitarska ~** *n.f.* guitar string
strup *n.m.* poison; **~en** *adj.* toxic
suh *adj.* thin, slim, skinny; dry
suròv *adj.* raw
sušíti *v.* to dry; **sušilec za lase** *n.m.* hair dryer
svak *n.m.* brother-in-law; **~ inja** *n.f.* sister-in-law
svátba *n.f.* wedding, marriage
svéča *n.f.* candle
svét *n.m.* world
svêt *n.m.* council (*admin.*)
svetlóba *n.f.* light
svéž *adj.* fresh
svíla *n.f.* silk; **svilen šal** *n.m.* silk scarf
svínčnik *n.m.* pencil

svinjína *n.f.* pork meat
svobôda *n.f.* freedom, liberty
svobôden *adj.* free

Š

šah *n.m.* chess
šal *n.m.* scarf
šála *n.f.* joke
šampánjec *n.m.* champagne
šampión *n.m.* ace, champion
šampón *n.m.* shampoo
šásija *n.f.* chassis (*autom.*)
ščétka *n.f.* brush
še *adv.* still, yet
šef *n.m.* boss, employer
šest *num.* six
šíbek *adj.* weak, fragile
šíren *adj.* wide, extended, spacious
šívati *v.* to sew
škárje *n.f.pl.* scissors
škóda *n.f.* damage; harm; **kakšna ~** *interj.* what a pity
šmínka *n.f.* lipstick
šôk *n.m.* shock
šóla *n.f.* school
šôtor *n.m.* tent; **~ za dve osebi** *n.m.* tent for two
šotóriti *v.* to camp
špeceríja *n.f.* grocery
špinâča *n.f.* spinach
šport *n.m.* sport; **~nik** *n.m.* athlete, jock
štedílnik *n.m.* cooker, stove
števílo *n.nt.* number; **poštna številka** *n.f.* zip code
štipéndija *n.f.* scholarship, grant
štíri *num.* six
štópati *v.* to hitchike
študént-ka *n.m.* student

študírati *v.* to study

šúnka *n.f.* ham

T

ta *pron.* this; this one, this here

tabléta *n.f.* pill, tablet

tabor *n.m.* camp; **~nik** *n.m.* scout

tajnik-ca *n.f.* secretary

takòj *adv.* at once, immediately; **~šen** *adj.* immediate, instant

takràt *adv.* at that time

táksi *n.m.* taxi, cab

tam *adv.* there

tarífa *n.f.* tariff, rate

tarók *n.m.* tarock (Hungarian card game)

tast *n.m.* father-in-law, **tášča** *n.f.* mother-in-law

tat *n.m.* thief, robber

tavêrna *n.f.* tavern

teáter *n.m.* theater

tečáj *n.m.* course; **jezikovni ~** *n.m.* language course

têči *v.* to run

téden *n.m.* week

téhnik *n.m.* technician

tehnologíja *n.m.* technology

tek *n.m.* appetite; **dober ~!** enjoy! (*culin.*)

tékma *n.f.* match, game

tekmovánje *n.nt.* competition, contest

tekóč *adj.* liquid

tekstíl *n.m.* textile; **~ na industrija** *n.f.* textile industry

telefón *n.m.* telephone

telefonírati *v.* to phone

telegrám *n.m.* telegram; **poslati ~** *v.* to send a telegram

teleskôp *n.m.* telescope

televizíja *n.f.* television; **gledati televizijo** *v.* to watch TV

telovádba *n.f.* gym, gymnastic; physical training

telóvnik *n.m.* vest

temèn *adj.* dark

temperatúra *n.f.* temperature

ténis *n.m.* tennis; **namizni ~** *n.m.* table tennis

terása *n.f.* terrace

termométer *n.m.* thermometer

têsen *adj.* narrow, tight

tést *n.m.* test, exam

testeníne *n.f.pl.* pasta

têta *n.f.* aunt

téža *n.f.* weight

težáva *n.f.* problem, difficulty, trouble

têžek *adj.* heavy; difficult, hard

ti *pron.* you (*sing.*)

tih *adj.* quiet, silent

típičen *adj.* typical, representative

tir *n.m.* rail

tísoč *num.* thousand

tíšína *n.f.* silence

tla *n.f.* floor, ground

to *pron.* this, that; **~ obleko** this dress

tóčen *adj.* punctual, precise

tok *n.m.* current, power, stream; **napetost električnega toka** *n.f.* voltage

tolmáč *n.m.* interpreter

tóna *n.f.* tone

tôpel *adj.* warm

toplíce *n.f.pl.* spa

tórba *n.f.* bag; **torbica** *n.f.* purse, handbag

tôrek *n.m.* Tuesday

tórta *n.f.* cake; **sadna ~** *n.f.* fruit cake

továrna *n.f.* factory

tôvor *n.m.* load, cargo

tradícija *n.f.* tradition

trafíka *n.f.* tobacco shop
trájanje *n.nt.* duration
trajékt *n.m.* car ferry
trák *n.m.* band, strip; **samolepilni** ~ *n.m.* self-adhesive tape
transpórt *n.m.* transport
tráva *n.f.* grass, lawn
trd *adj.* hard, stiff, firm, solid
trébuh *n.m.* stomach
trenér *n.m.* coach, trainer
trenútek *n.m.* moment, while
trepálnica *n.f.* eyelash
trésti *v.* to shake
trétji *num.* third
trèzen *adj.* sober
trg *n.m.* market; **~ovec** *n.m.* trader; **~ovína** *n.f.* shop; trade, commerce
tri *num.* three
trikótnik *n.m.* triangle
tŕkati *v.* to knock
trobénta *n.f.* trumpet
trôbilo *n.nt.* horn (*autom.*)
trud *n.m.* effort, hard work
tu, túkaj *adv.* here
túdi *adv.* too, also, as well
tuj *adj.* foreign, strange, unknown
tújec *n.m.* stranger, foreigner, alien
tujína *n.f.* foreign country; abroad, overseas
túkaj *adv.* here
túnel *n.m.* tunnel
turíst *n.m.* tourist

U

ubíti *v.* to kill, to murder; to assassinate
účbenik *n.m.* study book, textbook

učénec *n.m.* pupil, student
učínek *n.m.* effect
učítelj *n.m.* teacher
učíti se *v.* to learn; to memorize
udáriti *v.* to hit, to punch
udóben *adj.* comfortable; **ne~** *adj.* uncomfortable
ugásniti *v.* to turn off, to switch off; to extinguish
uhó *n.nt.* ear
ujéti *v.* to catch, to capture
ukáz *n.m.* order
úlica *n.f.* street
umázan *adj.* dirty, filthy
uméten *adj.* artificial
umétnik *n.m.* artist; **umetnica** *n.f.* artist
umétnost *n.f.* art
umiváti *v.* to wash
umiválnik *n.m.* sink
umôr *n.m.* murder
umréti *v.* to die, to pass away
únča *n.f.* ounce (28.35 gr)
unifórma *n.f.* uniform
univérza *n.f.* university
úpati *v.* to hope, to expect
uplinjáč *n.m.* carburetor (*autom.*)
upokójen *adj.* retired
uporábljati *v.* to use; **uporábnik** *n.m.* user
upráva *n.f.* administration, management
uprávnik *n.m.* administrator, manager
úra *n.f.* hour; watch; clock
uredíti *v.* to arrange, to take care of
uredník *n.m.* editor
úrnik *n.m.* schedule, timetable
uslúga *n.f.* favor
usmériti *v.* to direct, to orientate; **pre~** *v.* to redirect
úsnje *n.nt.* leather
uspèh *n.m.* success, victory
ústa *n.f.pl.* mouth; **ustnica** *n.f.* lip

ustanóva *n.f.* institution, establishment; **javna** ~ *n.f.* public institution
ustáviti *v.* to stop
ušésa *n.f.pl.* ears
utrújen *adj.* tired
uvážati *v.* to import
uvód *n.m.* introduction
uvóz *n.m.* import; **uvozni davek** *n.m.* import tax
užívati *v.* to enjoy

V

v *prep.* in, at, into, to
vabílo *n.nt.* invitation
vagón *n.m.* wagon
vája *n.f.* exercise
valj *n.m.* cylinder
valúta *n.f.* currency; **tuja** ~ *n.f.* foreign currency
váren *adj.* safe, secure
varováti *v.* to protect
várščina *n.f.* deposit
váruška *n.f.* baby-sitter, nanny
vas *n.f.* village
vat *n.m.* watt
vážen *adj.* important, significant
včásih *adv.* sometimes
včéraj *adv.* yesterday
vdóva *n.f.* widow; **vdovec** *n.m.* widow
več *adv.* more, several
večér *n.m.* eve, evening; **dober** ~**!** *interj.* good evening!
večerja *n.f.* dinner, supper; **večerjati** *v.* to dine
večína *n.f.* majority
véčji *adj.* bigger, larger
védeti *v.* to know
védno *adv.* always, constantly, ever

vegetarijánec *n.m.* vegetarian

vek *n.m.* age, epoch, era; **Srednji ~** *n.m.* Middle Ages

veleblagóvnica *n.f.* supermarket, department store

veleposlánik *n.m.* ambassador

veleposláništvo *n.nt.* embassy

vêlik *adj.* big, tall, large, grand; **Velika noč** *n.f.* Easter

velíko *adv.* much, a lot

velikóst *n.f.* size, dimension

veljáven *adj.* valid; **~ do** valid until

ven *adv.* out

véra *n.f.* faith, religion

veríga *n.f.* chain; **snežna ~** *n.f.* snow chain (*autom.*)

verjéti *v.* to believe, to trust

ves *adj.* all, whole

vesél *adj.* happy, jolly, glad

vesólje *n.m.* space, universe

véter *n.m.* wind

veterínar *n.m.* veterinarian

vezálke *n.f.pl.* shoelaces

véznik *n.m.* conjunction (*gram.*)

vhód *n.m.* entrance, way in

vi *pron.* you (*pl.*); you (*form.*)

videokamera *n.m.* camcorder

vídeti *v.* to see; **se vidimo!** *interj.* see you!

vihár *n.m.* storm

vijóličen *adj.* purple (*col.*)

vílice *n.f.pl.* fork

víno *n.nt.* wine; **vinógrad** *n.m.* vineyard

violína *n.f.* violin

víski *n.m.* whiskey

visôk *adj.* tall, high

višína *n.f.* altitude

vitamín *n.m.* vitamin

vítek *adj.* thin, slim

vizítka *n.f.* business card

vízum *n.m.* visa; **~ za večkratni vstop** *n.m.*
    multiple-entry visa

vključen *adj.* included; **vključeno v ceno** *adj.* included in the price

vkŕcati (se) *v.* to board, to embark

vláda *n.f.* government

vlága *n.f.* dampness, humidity, moistness

vlak *n.m.* train

vnétje *n.nt.* inflammation

vnuk *n.m.* grandson; ~ **inja** *n.f.* granddaughter

vnúki *n.m.pl.* grandchildren

vôda *n.f.* water

vodíti *v.* to guide, to lead; **vodič po Balkanu** *n.m.* Balkan tourist guide

vodník *n.m.* guide, leader

vodnják *n.m.* fountain

vódoraven *adj.* horizontal

vogál *n.m.* corner, turn

voják *n.m.* soldier

vôjna *n.f.* war

vólja *n.f.* will, spirit; humor

vôlna *n.f.* wool; **volnen pulover** *n.m.* woolen sweater

vónj *n.m.* scent, smell

vósek *n.m.* wax

vóščiti *v.* to wish, to congratulate

vôzel *n.m.* knot

vozíček *n.m.* trolley

vozílo *n.nt.* vehicle

vozíti *v.* to drive; **voznik** *n.m.* driver, chauffeur

vozóvnica *n.f.* ticket; **voznína** *n.f.* fare

vpisáti *v.* to register

vpliv *n.m.* influence

vprašánje *n.nt.* question, query; **vprašalnik** *n.m.* questionnaire

vprášati *v.* to ask, to interrogate

vrat *n.m.* neck

vráta *n.f.* door, gate

vŕč *n.m.* jug

vréča *n.f.* bag; **spalna ~** *n.f.* sleeping bag

vrême *n.nt.* weather

vrh *n.m.* top

vrhóvni *adj.* supreme; **vrhovno sodišče** *n.nt.* supreme court

vrniti *v.* to return, to give back

vróč *adj.* hot

vročíca *n.f.* fever, heat

vŕsta *n.f.* kind, type; queue, row

vrt *n.m.* garden

vŕtnica *n.f.* rose

vrtogláv *adj.* dizzy

vrv *n.f.* cord, rope

vsak *adj.* every, each; **~danji** *adj.* daily

vse *adv.* all, everything; **~ najboljše!** *interj.* happy birthday!

vsebína *n.f.* contents; stuffing (*culin.*)

vsebováti *v.* to contain

vsi *pron.* everybody

vstopíti *v.* to enter

vstópnica *n.f.* entrance ticket, admission ticket

vstopnína *n.f.* admission, entrance fee, registration fee

vtikáč *n.m.* plug

vzéti *v.* to take

vzdolž *adv.* along

vzdrževánje *n.nt.* maintenance

vzhod *n.m.* east; **V~na Evropa** *n.f.* Eastern Europe

vznemirljív *adj.* exciting

vzórec *n.m.* sample, pattern

vzrôk *n.m.* cause, reason

vžig *n.m.* ignition (*autom.*); **~alnik** *n.m.* lighter

Z

z/s *conj.* with, along with, in the company of; from

za *prep.* for, because; behind

zabáva *n.f.* fun, party, celebration
zabáven *adj.* amusing, funny
zabôj *n.m.* chest, case, box
začásen *adj.* temporal; **začasno bivališče** *n.nt.* temporary residence
začéti *v.* to start, to begin
začímbe *n.f.pl.* spices
zadéva *n.f.* affair, matter, issue
zádnji *adj.* last
zadovóljen *adj.* satisfied
zadŕga *n.f.* zipper, zip fastener
zahôd *n.m.* west; **zahoden** *adj.* western
zahtévati *v.* to require, to demand
zahvála *n.f.* thanks
zájec *n.m.* rabbit
zájtrk *n.m.* breakfast
zajtrkováti *v.* to have breakfast
zakáj *pron.* why, for what reason
zakleníti *v.* to lock
zákon *n.m.* marriage, matrimony
zalív *n.m.* bay, gulf
zaménjati *v.* to change
zamúda *n.f.* delay
zamudíti *v.* to miss, to be late, to delay
zanimív *adj.* interesting
zapéstje *n.nt.* wrist
zapéstnica *n.f.* bracelet; **zapestni gumbi** *n.m.pl.* cuff links
zapisáti *v.* to write (down)
zapór *n.m.* jail, prison
zaposlítev *n.f.* employment, job, occupation
zapréti *v.* to close, to shut down
zapŕto *adj.* closed
zaračúnati *v.* to charge
zarádi *conj.* because of, owing to
zaročên *adj.* engaged
zasében *adj.* private

zaslòn *n.m.* display, screen
zaslúžiti *v.* to earn, to win
zaspán *adj.* sleepy
zastáva *n.f.* flag
zastónj *adv.* free, gratis
zaščítiti *v.* to protect
zató *conj.* therefore
zaúpanje *n.nt.* trust
zavarovánje *n.nt.* insurance
zavésa *n.f.* curtain
zavetíšče *n.nt.* shelter
zavíti *v.* to turn; to wrap up
zavóra *n.f.* brake; **ročna ~** *n.f.* handbrake (*autom.*)
zavrtéti (številko) *v.* to dial (a number)
zbírati *v.* to collect, to gather
zbírka *n.f.* collection
zbógom! *interj.* goodbye!
zbórnica *n.f.* chamber; **gospodarska ~** *n.f.* chamber
  of commerce
zbúditi se *v.* to wake up
zdaj *adv.* now, currently
zdravílo *n.nt.* cure, medicine
zdráviti *v.* to cure, to heal
zdrávje *n.nt.* health
zdravník *n.m.* doctor; **zdravniški pregled** *n.m.*
  medical exam
zdrúženje *n.nt.* association, organization
zébra *n.f.* zebra
zelèn *adj.* green (*col.*)
zelenjáva *n.f.* vegetable
zelíšče *n.nt.* herb, plant
zélje *n.nt.* cabbage
zeló *adv.* very, highly
zêmlja *n.f.* earth, land, soil
zemljevíd *n.m.* map
zêt *n.m.* son-in-law
zgódba *n.f.* story, fairy tale

zgodíti se *v.* to happen, to occur
zgódnji *adj.* early
zgodovína *n.f.* history
zgôraj *prep.* above, up, upstairs
zgradíti *v.* to build, to construct
zgrádba *n.f.* construction, building
zid *n.m.* wall
zíma *n.f.* winter
zjútraj *adv.* in the morning; **jutri** ~ *adv.* tomorrow
    morning
zlásti *adv.* especially, above all
zlató *n.nt.* gold
zlo *n.nt.* evil
zmága *n.f.* victory
zmágati *v.* to win
zmaj *n.m.* dragon
zmánjšati *v.* decrease, reduce
zmêden *adj.* confused
zmének *n.m.* date
zméraj *prep.* always
zmóžen *adj.* able, capable
zmŕzniti *v.* to freeze; **zmrznjena hrana** *n.f.* frozen
    food
znáčka *n.f.* badge
znak *n.m.* sign, signal
znamenít *adj.* famous, well-known
známenje *n.nt.* sign, mark
známka *n.f.* stamp
znan *adj.* known, familiar
znánje *n.nt.* knowledge
znánost *n.f.* science
znánstvenik *n.m.* scientific
znáti *v.* to know, to be able
zob *n.m.* tooth; **~obol** *n.m.* toothache; **~ozdravnik,**
    ~ar *n.m.* dentist
zobotrèbec *n.m.* toothpick
zoo *n.m.* zoo

zrak *n.m.* air
zrel *adj.* mature
zrézek *n.m.* steak, fillet; **goveji** ~ *n.m.* beefsteak
zúnaj *adv.* out, outside
zúnanji *adj.* external, outdoors
zvečér *adv.* in the evening
zvéza *n.f.* union, association, league
zvézda *n.f.* star
zvézek *n.m.* notebook
zvóčnik *n.m.* loudspeaker
zvok *n.m.* sound, tone

Ž

žába *n.f.* frog
žálosten *adj.* sad
žámet *n.m.* velvet; ~ **na obleka** *n.f.* velvet dress
žárnica *n.f.* bulb
že *adv.* already
žébelj *n.m.* nail
žéjen *adj.* thirsty
želé *n.m.* jelly
želéti *v.* to wish, to want, to desire
želéznica *n.f.* railway
želézo *n.nt.* iron
žêlja *n.f.* wish, desire
želódec *n.m.* stomach
žélva *n.f.* turtle
žêna *n.f.* wife
žénska *n.f.* woman
žep *n.m.* pocket; ~**ni nož** *n.m.* pocketknife
žetón *n.m.* token
žíca *n.f.* wire, cable
žičnica *n.f.* cable car
žid *n.m.* Jew
žig *n.m.* rubber stamp

žíla *n.f.* vein
žíto *n.nt.* cereal
živ *adj.* alive
živéti *v.* to live
živál *n.f.* animal; **domača** ~ *n.f.* pet
žívjo! *interj.* hi! hello!
življénje *n.nt.* life
žlíca *n.f.* spoon
žóga *n.f.* ball
župán *n.m.* major
žužélka *n.f.* bug, insect
žvéčiti *v.* to chew; **žvečilni gumi** *n.m.* chewing gum

English-Slovene Dictionary

A

a *adj.* en, eden
abbey *n.* prepad
able *adj.* zmožen, sposoben
aboard *adv.* na ladji, na krovu, na palubi, v letalu
about *prep.* o; približno, okoli
above *adv.* nad
abroad *adv.* v tujini, zunaj, daleč
absolutely *adv.* seveda, popolnoma, povsem
academy *n.* akademija; **music ~** *n.* glasbena akademija
accelerate *v.* pospešiti
accent *n.* naglas, poudarek; *v.* naglasiti, poudariti
accept *v.* sprejeti, dopustiti
access *n.* dostop
accessories *n.* dodatek, dodatni pribor; pripomoček
accident *n.* nesreča, pripetljaj; slučaj; **car ~** *n.* prometna nesreča
accommodation *n.* prenočišče, nastanitev
accompany *v.* spremljati
account *n.* račun, konto; **bank ~** *n.* bančni račun
ache *n.* bolečina; **head~** *n.* glavobol; **tooth~** *n.* zobobol
achieve *v.* doseči; **to ~ a goal** *v.* doseči cilj
acid *n.* kislina; *adj.* kisel
acknowledge *v.* priznati, potrditi
acoustic *adj.* akustičen; **~ guitar** *n.* akustična kitara
across *prep.* prek, čez; križema; **~ the road** čez cesto
act *n.* dejanje; listina; *v.* igrati, predstavljati; **company ~** *n.* družbena pogodba
action *n.* dejanje, delovanje, učinek
activity *n.* dejavnost

actor *n.* igralec; **lead** ~ *n.* glavni igralec
actress *n.* igralka
adapter *n.* polnilnik
address *n.* naslov; *v.* nasloviti, nagovoriti
adhesive tape *n.* samolepilni trak
adjective *n.* pridevnik
administration *n.* uprava, upravljanje; **public** ~ *n.*
  javna uprava
admission *n.* včlanjenje; ~ **charge** *n.* vstopnina
Adriatic Sea *n.* Jadransko morje
adult *adj.* odrasel, polnoleten
advantage *n.* prednost, ugodnost
advertisement *n.* naznanilo, oglas; reklama
advice *n.* nasvet; predlog
affair *n.* stvar, zadeva, afera
afford *v.* privoščiti si, nuditi
afraid *adj.* prestrašen, boječ; *v.* bati se
after *adv.* potem, po; kasneje
afternoon *n.* popoldne; **good** ~! dober dan!
aftershave *n.* losjon po britju
again *adv.* ponovno, še enkrat; drugič
against *conj.* proti
age *n.* starost; era, doba, vek
agency *n.* agencija; **press** ~ *n.* tiskovna agencija
agent *n.* agent; predstavnik, zastopnik
ago *adj.* minul, nekdanji; **a week** ~ pred enim
  tednom
agree (with) *v.* privoliti (v), strinjati se (s/z)
agreement *n.* sporazum, dogovor
agriculture *n.* poljedelstvo, kmetijstvo
ahead *adv.* naprej, dalje, spredaj
aid *n.* pomoč; **first** ~ *n.* prva pomoč
aim *n.* cilj, namera
air *n.* zrak
air conditioning *n.* klimatska naprava
airmail *n.* zračna pošta, letalska pošta
air mattress *n.* zračna blazina

airplane *n.* avion, letalo

airport *n.* letališče; **international** ~ *n.* mednarodno letališče

alarm *n.* preplah; alarmna naprava, alarm; ~ **clock** *n.* budilka

album *n.* album; **photo** ~ *n.* foto album

alcohol *n.* alkohol

alcohol-free *adj.* brezalkoholen

alcoholic *adj.* alkoholen; ~ **drink** *n.* alkoholna pijača

alien *n.* tujec, vesoljec

alike *adj.* podoben, enak

alive *adj.* živ; živahen

all *adj.* vse, vsi, celoten; *adv.* popolnoma, povsem

allergic (to) *v.* biti alergičen na nekaj

allow *v.* dovoliti, dopustiti

almond *n.* mandelj

almost *adv.* skoraj

alone *adj.* sam; *adv.* samo, le

along *adv.* vzdolž, preko; ~ **the street** po cesti

alphabet *n.* abeceda

Alps *n.* Alpe; **Julian** ~ *n.* Julijske Alpe

already *adv.* že

also *adv.* tudi

although *conj.* čeprav

altitude *n.* višina, globina

always *adv.* vselej, vsakokrat, vedno

A.M. *prep.* dopoldne

amateur *n.* amater

ambassador *n.* ambasador

ambulance *n.* rešilni avto

among *prep.* med, izmed

amount *n.* vsota, količina, vrednost

amphibian *n.* dvoživka

amuse *v.* zabavati

anchor *n.* sidro

ancient *adj.* starodaven, starinski

and *conj.* in, ter, pa

anecdote *n.* anekdota
angel *n.* angel
angle *n.* kot
angry *adj.* jezen, razdražen
animal *n.* žival
anise *n.* janež
ankle *n.* gleženj; **to sprain one's** ~ *v.* izpahniti si
   gleženj
anniversary *n.* obletnica, jubilej
another *adj.* drug, drugačen, še eden
answer *n.* odgovor, odziv
ant *n.* mravlja
antenna *n.* antena
anthem *n.* himna; **national** ~ *n.* narodna himna
antifreeze *n.* protizmrzovalno sredstvo
antiquaries *n.* antikvariat, starinarnica
antique *n.* starinski, staromoden
anxious *adj.* zaskrbljen, nestrpen
any *adv.* karkoli
anyone *pron.* vsakdo, kdo, kdorkoli
anything *pron.* karkoli, vse
anyway *adv.* kakorkoli, nekoliko
anywhere *adv.* povsod, kjerkoli
apartment *n.* stanovanje, apartma; **one-bedroom** ~
   n. enosobno stanovanje
apologize *v.* opravičiti se
appetite *n.* apetit, tek; **bon appetit!** dober tek!
apple *n.* a jabolko; ~ **tree** *n.* jablana; ~ **pie** *n.*
   jabolčna pita
apply *v.* položiti, prilepiti, uporabiti; prijaviti se
appointment *n.* določitev; domenek, sestanek
approximately *adv.* približno, skoraj
apricot *n.* marelica; ~ **jam** *n.* marelična marmelada
April *n.* april; ~ **fool** *n.* aprilska šala
aquarium *n.* akvarij
arch *n.* lok
archaic *adj.* arhaičen, starinski

archeologist *n.* arheolog
archeology *n.* arheologija
architect *n.* arhitekt
architecture *n.* arhitektura
area *n.* področje, površina
argue *v.* prepirati se, diskutirati; dokazovati
arm *n.* roka; naročje
armchair *n.* naslanjač
army *n.* armada, vojska
around *adv.* okoli, naokoli; približno
arrange *v.* razporediti, urediti, pripraviti
arrival *n.* prihod
arrive *v.* priti, prispeti, dospeti
arrow *n.* puščica
art *n.* umetnost, veda, veščina; ~ **gallery** *n.* umetnostna
  galerija
artichoke *n.* artičoka
article *n.* člen; članek; predmet, blago
artificial *adj.* umeten, izumetničen
artist *n.* umetnik
as *adv.* kot, tako kot; *conj.* kot, koliko, ker
ash *n.* pepel; ruševine
ashtray *n.* pepelnik
ask *v.* vprašati; povabiti; zahtevati
asparagus *n.* beluš
aspirin *n.* aspirin
assistant *n.* asistent, pomočnik
association *n.* združenje, društvo, zveza
asthma *n.* astma, naduha
astrology *n.* astrologija
asylum *n.* azil; **political** ~ *n.* politični azil
atheist *n.* ateist
athletics *n.* atletika
atlas *n.* atlas; **world** ~ *n.* atlas sveta
atmosphere *n.* atmosfera; vzdušje
attaché *n.* ataše
attend *v.* paziti; skrbeti; obiskovati

attention *n.* pozornost, oskrba, nega; ~! pozôr!
attractive *adj.* privlačen, vabljiv, očarljiv
audience *n.* občinstvo, publika
August *n.* avgust
aunt *n.* teta
authentic *adj.* avtentičen, pravi
author *n.* avtor, pisec
authority *n.* avtoriteta; oblast
automatic *adj.* avtomatičen, samodéjen
autumn *n.* jesen
available *adj.* na razpolago, razpoložljiv; uporaben
avalanche *n.* plaz, lavina
avenue *n.* avenija, dohod
average *adj.* povprečen, srednji, običajen
avocado *n.* avokado
avoid *v.* izogibati se
awake *adj.* zbujen, buden
award *n.* nagrada
away *adv.* proč, stran; **right** ~ takoj
awful *adj.* grozen, strašen

B

baby *n.* dojenček, otročiček; dragi; ~ **food** *n.* otroška
  hrana; **baby-sitter** *n.* varuška
bachelor *n.* samski, neporočen moški
back *n.* hrbet, zadnja stran; *adv.* nazaj, zadaj
backpack *n.* nahrbtnik, oprtnik
bacon *n.* slanina; **eggs with** ~ *n.* jajca z slanino
bad *adj.* slab, pokvarjen, škodljiv; ~ **mood** *n.* slaba
  volja, slabo razpoloženje
badge *n.* značka
badger *n.* jazbec
bag *n.* vreča, torba, kovček; *v.* ujeti, dati v vrečo
baggage *n.* prtljaga
bake *v.* peči (se)

baker *n.* pek
bakery *n.* pekarna
balcony *n.* balkon
bald *adj.* plešast
ball *n.* žoga, klopčič;
ballet *n.* balet; ~ **dancer** *n.* baletnik (*m.*), balerina (*f.*)
balloon *n.* balon
banana *n.* banana; ~ **tree** *n.* bananovec
band *n.* trak; orkester
bandage *n.* obveza, povoj; ~ **box** *n.* omarica za prvo pomoč
bank *n.* banka; klop; jarek
banknote *n.* bankovec
baptism *n.* krst (*relig.*)
bar *n.* bar; palica, drog
barber *n.* brivec
bargain *v.* barantati, pogajati se
bark *v.* lajati
barman *n.* natakar, točaj
baron *n.* baron
baroque *n.* barok; *adj.* baročen; ~ **style** *n.* baročni stil
barrier *n.* ovira; ograja; pregrada
base *n.* osnova, podlaga, temelj; baza (*milt.*)
basement *n.* klet; prizemlje
basil *n.* bazilika (*culin.*)
basilica *n.* bazilika (*relig.*)
basket *n.* koš, košara
basketball *n.* košarka
bastard *n.* baraba (*insult.*)
bat *n.* netopir
bath *n.* kopel, kad
bathe *v.* kopati se, umivati se
bathroom *n.* kopalnica, stranišče
bathtub *n.* kopalna kad
battery *n.* baterija; **car** ~ *n.* akumulator
bay *n.* zaliv; jez
be *v.* biti

beach *n.* obala, plaža, peščina
bean *n.* fižol; zrno
bear *n.* medved; *v.* nositi; prenesti, prenašati; **to ~ a child** *v.* biti noseča
beard *n.* brada
beast *n.* zver, zverina (*zool.*)
beat *n.* udarec, bitje, utrip, ritem; *v.* udarjati, tolči, biti, premagati
beautiful *adj.* lep, krasen
beauty *n.* lepota; lepotica
because *conj.* ker, zato ker; **~ of** zaradi
become *v.* postati, nastati
bed *n.* postelja, ležišče; **~clothes** *n.* posteljnina
bedroom *n.* spalnica; **single ~** *n.* spalnica z eno posteljo
bee *n.* čebela
beech *n.* bukev
beef *n.* govedina; **~steak** *n.* goveji zrezek, biftek
beer *n.* pivo
before *adv.* prej, preden; spredaj
beg *v.* beračiti, prositi, rotiti
beggar *n.* berač, revež
begin *v.* začeti, pričeti, lotiti se
beginning *n.* začetek, nastanek; izvor
behind *prep.* zadaj, za
believe (in) *v.* verjeti (v); zaupati; misliti
bell *n.* zvonec
bellybutton *n.* popek
belong *v.* pripadati, spadati
below *adv.* spodaj, niže
belt *n.* pas, jermen; **seat~** *n.* varnostni pas
bench *n.* klop, delovna miza
bend *v.* upogniti, prepogniti
benefit *n.* korist, ugodnost; v dobro
beside *prep.* razen; poleg, ob strani
best *adj.* najboljši, najprimernejši
better *adj.* bolje, boljši, primernejši

between *prep.* med; ~ **us** med nama
beverage *n.* pijača; **non-alcoholic** ~ *n.*
brezalkoholna pijača
beyond *adv.* na drugi strani, onstran, preko
Bible *n.* Biblija
bicycle *n.* kolo; **to ride a** ~ *v.* kolesariti
big *adj.* velik, važen; odrasel
bilingual *adj.* dvojezičen
bill *n.* račun; seznam; bankovec; ~ **of health** *n.*
zdravniško spričevalo
bin *n.* zaboj, košara, posoda; **dust~** *n.* koš za smeti
bind *v.* povezati, vezati
bird *n.* ptica, ptič
birth *n.* rojstvo, porod; nastanek; ~ **certificate** *n.*
rojstni list
birthday *n.* rojstni dan
biscuit *n.* prepečenec, keks
bit *n.* drobec, kos, košček; grižljaj
bite *v.* gristi, odgristi
bitter *adj.* grenek, trpek, bridek
black *n.* črn; ~ **person** *n.* črnec
blackberries *n.* črni ribez
blade *n.* nož, rezilo
bladder *n.* mehur
blanket *n.* odeja, prevleka; **woolen** ~ *n.* volnena odeja
blazon *n.* grb
bleach *n.* belilo; *v.* beliti, pobeliti
blind *adj.* slep
blister *n.* žulj, mehurček
blizzard *n.* snežni vihar, metež
block *n.* blok, zastoj; *v.* blokirati, zagraditi
blood *n.* kri; ~ **group** *n.* krvna skupina
blouse *n.* bluza
blow *v.* pihati; razstreliti
blue *n.* modra, plava; modrina
board *n.* deska, plošča, tabla; **~ing pass** *n.* vstopni
karton
boat *n.* čoln; **sail~** *n.* jadrnica

body *n.* telo, truplo; jedro
boil *v.* vreti, kuhati v vreli vodi, zavreti; **~ed eggs** *n.* kuhana jajca
bone *n.* kost, koščica
book *n.* knjiga, zvezek; *v.* rezervirati, vknjižiti
bookcase *n.* knjižna omara
booking *n.* prodaja/rezervacija vozovnic
bookshop *n.* knjigarna
boots *n.* škornji
border *n.* rob, meja; **national ~** *n.* državna meja
boredom *n.* dolgčas
born *v.* roditi se
borrow *v.* izposoditi
boss *n.* šef, nadrejeni
both *pron.* oba
bother *v.* nadlegovati, motiti
bottle *n.* steklenica
bottom *n.* dno
box *n.* škatla, zaboj; **~ office** *n.* gledališka blagajna
boy *n.* fant; **little ~** *n.* fantek
boyfriend *n.* fant
bra *n.* nedrček, modrček
bracelet *n.* zapestnica
brain *n.* možgani
brake *n.* zavora
branch *n.* veja; podružnica
brand *n.* zaščitna znamka, marka
brandy *n.* vinjak
bread *n.* kruh; **white ~** *n.* bel kruh
break *v.* zlomiti, odlomiti, prelomiti
breakdown *n.* okvara (*autom.*)
breakfast *n.* zajtrk; **~ included** zajtrk vključen
breast *n.* prsi, dojka
breathe *n.* sapa; *v.* dihati, vdihavati
bride *n.* nevesta
bridge *n.* most, brv

brief *adj.* kratek, jedrnat
briefcase *n.* aktovka
bright *adj.* svetel, jasen
bring *v.* prinesti
broad *adj.* širok, obsežen
broadcast *n.* oddajanje; radijska oddaja
brochure *n.* brošura
broil *v.* pražiti se
broken *adj.* zlomljen, v okvari
bronze *n.* bron; ~ **medal** *n.* bronasta medalja
broom *n.* metla
broth *n.* juha
brother *n.* brat; ~-**in-law** *n.* svak
brown *n.* rjav
bruise *n.* odrgnina, poškodba
brush *n.* krtača, ščetka; **tooth~** *n.* zobna ščetka
Brussels *n.* Bruselj
bucket *n.* vedro, čeber
buckwheat *n.* ajda
bug *n.* hrošč (*zool.*, *autom.*); žuželka
build *v.* graditi, zidati, tvoriti
building *n.* stavba, zgradba, poslopje
bulb *n.* žarnica; čebulica, gomolj
bull *n.* bik; ~**fighting** *n.* bikoborba
bumper *n.* odbijač
bun *n.* žemlja, kruhek; šop
bunch *n.* svežnj, šopek, kup; **a ~ of people** *n.* gruča
  ljudi
bungalow *n.* bungalov
bureau de change *n.* menjalnica
burn *v.* goreti; zažgati
burst *v.* razpočiti, izbruhniti
bus *n.* avtobus; ~ **stop** *n.* avtobusna postaja
business *n.* posel, opravilo, poslovanje, delo
busy *adj.* delaven, marljiv, zaposlen; zaseden
but *conj.* ampak, toda, pač; *prep.* razen
butcher *n.* mesar, klavec

butter *n.* maslo
butterfly *n.* metulj
button *n.* gumb
buy *v.* kupiti; **good** ~ *n.* ugoden nakup
by *prep.* blizu, ob, od, do; *adv.* blizu, poleg; ~ **the bed** ob postelji
bye *interj.* adijo
by-way *n.* stranska pot

C

cab *n.* taksi
cabbage *n.* zelje, ohrovt
cabin *n.* koča
cable *n.* kabel, vrv; ~ **car** *n.* žičnica, gondola
cactus *n.* kaktus
café *n.* kava; ~ **au lait** *n.* kava z mlekom
cafeteria *n.* samopostrežna restavracija
cake *n.* kolač, torta; pecivo; **chocolate** ~ *n.* čokoladna torta
calcium *n.* kalcij
calendar *n.* kolendar
call *n.* klic; *v.* klicati, imenovati; ~ **me!** pokliči me!
calm *adj.* miren, spokojen
calorie *n.* kalorija
camcorder *n.* videokamera
camel *n.* kamela
camera *n.* fotoaparat
camp *n.* kamp, tabor, šotorišče; *v.* taboriti; ~**fire** *n.* taborniški ogenj
can *n.* konzerva; ~ **opener** *n.* odpirač
can *v.* moči; ~ **I…?** ali lahko…?, ali smem…?
cancel *v.* odpovedati
cancellation *n.* odpoved
candle *n.* sveča
candy *n.* sladkorček, bombon

canned *adj.* konzerviran
canoe *n.* kanu
cap *n.* čepica, kapa, pokrivalo
capital *adj.* glaven; ~ **city** *n.* glavno mesto,
  prestolnica
capitalism *n.* kapitalizem
captain *n.* kapitan
car *n.* avto; ~**wash** *n.* avtopralnica; ~ **ferry** *n.*
  trajekt; ~ **park** *n.* parkirišče
caravan *n.* karavana; avtodom
carburetor *n.* uplinjač
card *n.* karta, izkaznica; **business** ~ *n.* vizitka
cardigan *n.* pletena jopica; brezrokavnik
care *n.* briga, skrb, nega; zaskrbljenost; *v.* skrbeti,
  negovati; marati
careful *adj.* previden, pozoren, skrben
careless *adj.* brezskrben, nemaren
cargo *n.* naklad, tovor
carpet *n.* preproga, tepih
carriage *n.* kočija, voz, vagon
carrier *n.* prevoznik; špediter (*trans.*)
carrot *n.* korenje
carry *v.* nositi, prenašati
cartoon *n.* risanka
case *n.* primer, zadeva; **suit**~ *n.* kovček
cash *n.* gotovina, denar; ~**box** *n.* blagajna
cashier *n.* blagajnik
casino *n.* kazino, igralnica
castle *n.* grad, trdnjava
castor oil *n.* ricinusovo olje
casualty *n.* ranjenec, poškodovanec
cat *n.* maček
catch *v.* ujeti, uloviti, dohiteti
category *n.* kategorija
catering *n.* katering
caterpillar *n.* gosenica
cathedral *n.* katedrala

Catholic *adj.* katoliški; ~ **school** *n.* katoliška šola
cauliflower *n.* cvetača, karfijola (*fam.*)
cause *n.* vzrok, motiv, namen
caution *n.* svarilo, opozorilo; ~! pozôr!
cave *n.* jama, votlina
ceiling *n.* strop
celebrate *v.* praznovati, slaviti, proslavljati
cellar *n.* klet; **wine** ~ *n.* vinska klet
cemetery *n.* pokopališče
center *n.* središče, sredina
centimeter *n.* centimeter
century *n.* stoletje
ceramics *n.* keramika
cereals *n.* kosmiči
certificate *n.* spričevalo, izkaz, potrdilo, certifikat
chain *n.* veriga, vrsta
chair *n.* stol, sedež; **wheel~** *n.* invalidski voziček
chairlift *n.* sedežnica
chairman *n.* predsednik, upravnik
chalet *n.* brunarica, koča
chamber *n.* soba, komora; urad; ~ **of commerce**
  gospodarska zbornica
chamomile *n.* kamilice
champagne *n.* šampanjec
champion *n.* as, prvak, zmagovalec; **~ship** *n.*
  prvenstvo
chance *n.* možnost, sreča; slučaj, verjetnost
change *v.* spremeniti, zamenjati; *n.* sprememba
changing room *n.* preoblačilnica
channel *n.* kanal, prekop
chapel *n.* kapela
chapter *n.* poglavje
character *n.* karakter, osebnost
charcoal *n.* oglje
charge *v.* zaračunati; nabiti
chartered flight *n.* čarter, čarterski polet
chassis *n.* šasija

chat *v.* klepetati; *n.* klepet
cheap *adj.* poceni, cenen
check *n.* ček; *v.* preveriti, kontrolirati; ~ **in** *v.* prijaviti se, vpisati se
cheek *n.* lice, obraz
cheers! *interj.* na zdravje!
cheese *n.* sir; **goat** ~ *n.* kozji sir
chemistry *n.* kemija
chemists *n.* lekarna
cherry *n.* češnja
chess *n.* šah
chest *n.* oprsje; skrinja
chestnut *n.* kostanj
chew *v.* žvečiti; premišljevati
chewing gum *n.* žvečilni gumi, žvečilka
chicken *n.* piščanec; ~ **pox** *n.* norice
chief *n.* načelnik, šef, predstojnik
child *n.* otrok, dete
childhood *n.* otroštvo
children *n.* otroci
chili *n.* čili
chocolate *n.* čokolada
choice *n.* izbira, izbor
choose *v.* izbirati
chop *v.* narezati
Christian *adj.* krščanski
Christmas *n.* Božič; ~ **Eve** *n.* Božični večer
church *n.* cerkev
cider *n.* mošt, jabolčnik
cigar *n.* cigara
cigarette *n.* cigareta
cinema *n.* kino
cinnamon *n.* cimet
circle *n.* krog, obroč; *v.* krožiti
circus *n.* cirkus
citizen *n.* meščan, državljan; ~**ship** *n.* državljanstvo
city *n.* mesto

claim *n.* zahteva; *v.* zahtevati, terjati
clarinet *n.* klarinet
class *n.* razred, kategorija; **first ~** *n.* prvi razred
classical *adj.* klasičen
claw *n.* krempelj (*zool.*)
clay *n.* glina
clean *adj.* čist, snažen, opran; *v.* čistiti, pospravljati
cleansing cream *n.* čistilna krema
clear *adj.* jasen, bister, čist
clerk *n.* prodajalec; uradnik
clever *adj.* pameten, bister, zvit
client *n.* stranka, klient
climate *n.* klima, podnebje
climb *v.* plezati, vzpenjati se
clinic *n.* klinika
clock *n.* ura; **at five o'~** ob petih
close *adj.* bližnji; zaupen; *v.* zapreti, končati
closed *adj.* zapŕto
clothes *n.* obleka, oblačila, perilo; **winter ~** *n.*
  zimska oblačila
cloud *n.* oblak; **~y weather** *n.* oblačno vreme
club *n.* klub; **basketball ~** *n.* košarkaški klub
coach *n.* trener; avtobus; drugi razred (v letalu)
coal *n.* premog
coast *n.* obala, breg, obrežje
coast guard *n.* obalna straža
coat *n.* plašč; **~ hanger** *n.* obešalnik
cocktail *n.* koktajl
cocoa *n.* kakao; **~ butter** *n.* kakavovo maslo
coffee *n.* kava; **~house** *n.* kavarna
coin *n.* kovanec
colander *n.* cedilo, sito
cold *adj.* hladen, mrzel; *n.* mraz; prehlad; **I have a ~**
  prehlajen-a sem
collar *n.* ovratnik
collect *v.* zbirati, pobirati
collection *n.* zbirka; **stamp ~** *n.* zbirka znamk

color *n.* barva
column *n.* steber; rubrika, stolpec; **sports** ~ *n.*
športna rubrika
comb *v.* glavnik
combination *n.* kombinacija
come *v.* priti, prihajati; ~ **back** *v.* vrniti se; ~ **in** *v.*
vstopiti
comedy *n.* komedija
comfortable *adj.* udoben, prijeten
commercial *adj.* trgovski, reklamen; *n.* reklama
commission *n.* komisija
communication *n.* komunikacija
communion *n.* obhajilo (*relig.*)
communism *n.* komunizem
company *n.* podjetje, družba
compartment *n.* predelek, oddelek; kupé
competition *n.* konkurenca; tekmovanje
complaint *n.* pritožba, tožba; **book of ~s** *n.* pritožna
knjiga
complete *adj.* popoln, kompleten; *v.* dopolniti
comprehensive *adj.* izčrpen, obširen, obsežen
compromise *n.* kompromis; prilagoditev
compulsory *adj.* obvezen, prisilen
computer *n.* računálnik; ~ **programmer** *n.*
računalniški programer
concert *n.* koncert
condition *n.* pogoj, okoliščina; stanje
condom *n.* kondom, prezervativ
conductor *n.* dirigent, zborovodja; sprevodnik
confectionery *n.* slaščičarna
conference *n.* konferenca, posvetovanje; ~
interpreter *n.* konferenčni tolmač
confirm *v.* potrditi, odobriti
confused *adj.* zmêden
congratulations! *interj.* vse najboljše! (*birthday*)
congress *n.* kongres; **international** ~ *n.* mednarodni
kongres

connect *v.* povezati, združiti
connection *n.* povezava, stik, zveza
construct *v.* graditi, zidati, sestaviti
construction *n.* gradnja; zgradba, poslopje, stavba
consulate *n.* konzulat
consumer *n.* potrošnik; **~ goods** *n.* potrošniško blago
contact *n.* stik, zveza; *v.* vzpostaviti stik, kontaktirati
contact lenses *n.* kontaktne leče
contagious *adj.* nalezljiv
contain *v.* vsebovati, obsegati, zadrževati
contemporary *adj.* sodoben
contents *n.* vsebina, prostornina
continent *n.* kontinent
contraception *n.* kontracepcija
contrary *adj.* nasproten
control *n.* nadzor, pregled; *v.* nadzirati
cook *n.* kuhar; *v.* kuhati
cooker *n.* kuhalnik
cool *adj.* hladen, svež; hladnokrven, miren
cooperation *n.* sodelovanje
copper *n.* baker
copy *n.* kopija, prepis; izvod; *v.* kopirati, odtisniti, prepisovati
cord *n.* vrv; **vocal ~s** *n.* glasilke
corn *n.* koruza; zrno
corner *n.* kot, vogal
correct *adj.* pravi, pravilen, spodoben; *v.* popraviti
corridor *n.* hodnik
cosmetics *n.* kozmetika, lepotila
cost *n.* strošek, cena; *v.* stati, velja; **how much does it ~?** koliko stane?
costume *n.* kostum, preobleka; noša
cottage *n.* koliba, koča
cotton *n.* bombaž; **~ wool** *n.* vata; surov bombaž
cough *n.* kašelj; *v.* kašljati
council *n.* svet, zbor; **city ~** *n.* mestni svet (*admin.*)
count *n.* grof; *v.* šteti, računati

country *n.* država, dežela; **in the ~side** na deželi
county *n.* okrožje, okraj
couple *n.* par, dvojica
coupon *n.* kupon
courier *n.* kurir, sel
course *n.* tek, potek; krožek, tečaj; **Slovene ~** *n.*
tečaj slovenščine
court *n.* dvorišče; sodišče (*law*)
cousin *n.* bratranec (*m.*), sestrična (*f.*)
cover *n.* platnica, pokrov; *v.* pokriti, prekriti
cow *n.* krava
crab *n.* rakovica
cracker *n.* kreker, slani keksi
crash *n.* karambol, trk, nesreča
crayfish *n.* jastog
crayon *n.* kreda
cream *n.* krema, smetana (*culin.*)
credit *n.* kredit, posojilo; **~ card** *n.* kreditna kartica
cricket *n.* kriket
crisis *n.* kriza
critic *n.* kritik
crocodile *n.* krokodil
cross *v.* križati; **~road** *n.* križišče
crossing *n.* prehod, zebra
crowd *n.* množica, gneča; *v.* prerivati se
crown *n.* krona
cruise *n.* križarjenje; *v.* križariti
crush *v.* drobiti; **~ed ice** *n.* drobljen led
crutch *n.* bergla
cry *n.* klic, jok; *v.* jokati, klicati, tarnati
crystal *n.* kristal
cube *n.* kocka; **ice ~** *n.* ledena kocka
cubic *adj.* kubičen; **~ meter** *n.* kubični meter
cuckoo *n.* kukavica
cucumber *n.* kumara
cuff links *n.* zapestni gumbi
culture *n.* kultura

cup *n.* skodelica, čaša
cupboard *n.* omara
cure *n.* zdravilo; *v.* zdraviti
curious *adj.* radoveden; poseben
currant *n.* rozina; **red** ~ *n.* rdeči ribez
currency *n.* obtok; tečaj, veljava; **foreign** ~ *n.* tuja valuta
current *adj.* dejanski, veljaven; *n.* tok (*mar.*)
curtain *n.* zavesa, zagrinjalo
curve *n.* krivulja
cushion *n.* blazina
custom *n.* navada, običaj
customer *n.* stranka
customs *n.* carina; ~ **fee** *n.* carinska dajatev
cut *n.* rez; *v.* rezati, sekati
cutlery *n.* pribor (*culin.*)
cycle *v.* kolesariti
cycling *n.* kolesarjenje
cyclist *n.* kolesar
cylinder *n.* cilinder, valj
cypress *n.* cipresa (*bot.*)
Cyrillic *n.* cirilica

D

daily *adj.* vsakdanji, dneven
dairy *n.* mlekarna; ~ **product** *n.* mlečni izdelek
damage *n.* škoda, (i)zguba
damp *n.* vlaga, mokrota; *adj.* vlažen, moker
dance *n.* ples; *v.* plesati
danger *n.* nevarnost, grožnja
dangerous *adj.* nevaren, tvegan
Danube *n.* Donava
dark *adj.* temen, temačen
date *n.* datum, rok; zmenek, sestanek; *v.* videti se z nekom

daughter *n.* hči, hčerka
daughter-in-law *n.* snaha
day *n.* dan; **all** ~ ves dan
day-by-day *adv.* podnevi
dead *adj.* mrtev; ~ **end** *n.* slepa ulica
deaf *adj.* gluh, naglušen
deal *n.* posel, dogovor, sporazum
dear *adj.* drag, dragocen; ljubljen
death *n.* smrt
debt *n.* dolg, obveznost
December *n.* december
decide *v.* odločiti se (za)
deck *n.* krov, paluba; ~ **chair** *n.* ležalnik
declaration *n.* izjava, deklaracija
declare *v.* prijaviti, razglasiti; ocariniti (*cust.*)
decrease *v.* (u)pasti, (z)mánjšati
deep *adj.* globok; temeljit
defect *n.* defekt, napaka, hiba
defend *v.* braniti, ščititi
degree *n.* stopnja, stopinja; **five** ~**s Celsius** pet
    stopinj celzija
delay *n.* odlog, zamuda; *v.* zamuditi, zakasniti
delicate *adj.* občutljiv, rahel
delicatessen *n.* delikatesa
deliver *v.* dostaviti
delivery *n.* dostava; **home** ~ *n.* dostava na dom
demand *n.* zahteva, prošnja; povpraševanje; *v.*
    povpraševati, zahtevati
democracy *n.* demokracija
dense *adj.* gost, kompakten
dentist *n.* zobozdravnik
department *n.* oddelek, področje
departure *n.* odhod
depend (on) *v.* biti odvisen (od)
deposit *n.* polog; *v.* položiti, odložiti
depth *n.* globina, prepad
describe *v.* opisati

desert *n.* puščava
design *n.* načrt, vzorec, kroj
desire *n.* želja; *v.* želeti
desk *n.* (pisalna) miza
dessert *n.* sladica, posladek (*culin.*)
destination *n.* namen, naslov, cilj, destinacija
detail *n.* podrobnost, posameznost
detergent *n.* čistilo
development *n.* razvoj, napredek
device *n.* naprava, priprava
diabetes *n.* sladkorna bolezen
diagnosis *n.* diagnoza
dial *v.* zavrteti (številko); ~ **tone** *n.* klicni znak
dialect *n.* dialekt, narečje
diamond *n.* diamant
diaper *n.* plenica
diarrhea *n.* diareja, driska
diary *n.* dnevnik; **to keep a** ~ *v.* pisati dnevnik
dictionary *n.* slovar; **pocket** ~ *n.* žepni slovar
die *v.* umreti; poginiti (*zool.*)
diet *n.* dieta
difference *n.* razlika
different *adj.* drugačen, različen
dine *v.* večerjati
dining room *n.* jedilnica
dinner *n.* večerja; ~ **jacket** *n.* smoking
diploma *n.* diploma
diplomat *n.* diplomat
direct *adj.* direkten, neposreden; *v.* uravnavati,
   usmeriti
direction *n.* smer; navodilo; **right** ~ *n.* prava smer
director *n.* direktor, šef, upravnik
dirty *adj.* umazan, blaten
disappear *v.* izginiti
discount *n.* popust, rabat, znižanje
discover *v.* odkriti, najti
discovery *n.* najdba, odkritje

discuss *v.* razpravljati
disease *n.* bolezen
disembark *v.* izkrcati se
dish *n.* posoda; jed
dislike *v.* ne marati, ne trpeti
display *n.* zaslon, ekran; izložba; *v.* pokazati,
   razkazovati
distance *n.* daljava, razdalja
district *n.* okoliš, okrožje, soseska
disturb *v.* motiti, begati, vznemirjati
divide *v.* deliti, razdeliti
divorce *n.* ločitev; *v.* ločiti se
dizzy *n.* vrtoglav, omotičen; **I feel** ~ vrti se mi
do *v.* delati, narediti; **I did the washing up** pomil-a
   sem posodo.
doctor *n.* doktor, zdravnik
document *n.* dokument, listina
dog *n.* pes, kuža (*coll.*)
dollar *n.* dolar; **American** ~ ameriški dolar;
   Australian ~ avstralski dolar
dolphin *n.* delfin
domestic *adj.* domač, hišen
domicile *n.* bivališče
donkey *n.* osel
door *n.* vrata, vhod; ~ **handle** *n.* kljuka
dose *n.* doza, količina, odmerek
double *adj.* dvojen, dvakraten; *v.* podvojiti
doubt *n.* dvom, pomislek
doughnut *n.* krof
down *n.* spodaj, doli, navzdol
downstairs *adv.* po stopnicah navzdol
dozen *n.* ducat, dvanajst
dragon *n.* zmaj
drama *n.* drama
draw *v.* risati; potegniti
drawer *n.* predal
dream *n.* sanje, sen; *v.* sanjati; sanjariti

dress *n.* obleka; *v.* obleči se
dressing *n.* omaka, nadev (*culin.*)
drink *n.* pijača; *v.* piti, popiti
drive *v.* voziti, peljati, pognati
driver *n.* voznik, šofer; gonilnik (*comp.*)
drop *v.* spustiti (se), izpustiti, pasti
drown *v.* utoniti, utopiti, potopiti
drug *n.* droga, mamilo, zdravilo
drugstore *n.* lekarna, drogerija
drunk *adj.* pijan
dry *adj.* suh, izsušen; *v.* sušiti
dry cleaner *n.* kemična čistilnica
dryer *n.* sušilec za lase
dual *n.* dvojina (*gram.*)
duck *n.* raca
dumpling *n.* cmok; **bread ~** *n.* kruhovi cmoki
    (*culin.*)
durable *adj.* dolgotrajen, trajen
duration *n.* trajanje
during *prep.* med; **~ the night** *adv.* ponoči
dusk *n.* mrak
dust *n.* prah
duty *n.* dolžnost, obveznost; davek
duty-free shop *n.* brezcarinska prodajalna
dynamo *n.* dinamo (*autom.*)

E

each *pron.* vsakdo; *adj.* vsak
ear *n.* uho; posluh
early *adj.* zgodnji, ran
earn *v.* pridobiti, zaslužiti (si)
earth *n.* zemlja, prst
east *n.* vzhod; **Far East** *n.* Daljni vzhod; **in the ~**
    adv. na vzhodu
Easter *n.* Velika noč; **~ eggs** *n.* pirhi

eastern *adj.* vzhoden
easy *adj.* lahek, lahkoten; brezskrben
eat *v.* jesti, pojesti; razjedati, uničiti
economical *adj.* ekonomski, gospodaren
economy *n.* ekonomija, gospodarstvo
education *n.* izobrazba, vzgoja
effect *n.* posledica, učinek
effort *n.* trud
egg *n.* jajce
eggplant *n.* jajčevec
eight *num.* osem
either *adj.* oba; *n.* kakorkoli, niti
elastic *n.* elastika; *adj.* elastičen
elbow *n.* komolec
electric *n.* elektrika
electrician *n.* električar
elementary *adj.* elementaren, osnoven; ~ **school** *n.*
    osnovna šola
elephant *n.* slon
elevator *n.* dvigalo
eleven *num.* enajst
else *adv.* drugje, drugače, še; **anywhere** ~ *adv.*
    kjerkoli drugje
embark *v.* vkrcati (se); natovoriti
embassy *n.* ambasada, veleposlaništvo
emergency *n.* nujnost, sila, potreba
empire *n.* imperij, cesarstvo
employment *n.* zaposlitev, posel, služba
empty *adj.* prazen; *v.* izprazniti
encyclopedia *n.* enciklopedija
end *n.* konec, zaključek; *v.* končati
energy *n.* energija; odločnost
engaged *adj.* zaročen; zaseden, oddan
engine *n.* motor, stroj
engineer *n.* inženir; **mechanical** ~ *n.* strojni inženir
enjoy *v.* uživati, zabavati se
enough *adv.* dovolj, zadosti

enter *v.* vstopiti; včlaniti se
entertainment *n.* zabava, razvedrilo
entire *adj.* ves, cel, celoten; ~ **day** cel dan
entrance *n.* vhod, vstop; ~ **fee** *n.* vstopnina
envelope *n.* kuverta
equal *adj.* enak, enakovreden
equipment *n.* oprema
error *n.* napaka, zmota, pomota
escalator *n.* tekoče stopnice
escape *v.* (u)bežati, pobegniti
especially *adv.* zlasti, predvsem
estate *n.* posest, zemljišče; **real** ~ *n.* nepremičnine
estimate *n.* ocena, mnenje; *v.* oceniti, presojati
etc. *abbrev.* itd. (in tako dalje)
ether *n.* eter
Europe *n.* Evropa; **European Union** *n.* Evropska
  Unija
eve *n.* večer (pred praznikom); **Christmas Eve** *n.*
  Božični večer
even *adj.* enak, paren; ~ **number** *n.* parno število
evening *n.* večer; **good** ~! dober večer!
event *n.* dogodek
ever *adv.* vedno, vselej, večno
everybody *n.* vsi, vsakdo; ~ **else** vsi drugi
everything *n.* vse
everywhere *adv.* povsod
evil *n.* zlo, hudobija
exact *adj.* natančen, točen
exam *n.* test, izpit
examination *n.* pregled, preiskava
example *n.* primer, vzorec, zgled; **for** ~ na primer
excellent *adj.* odličen, izvrsten
except *conj.* razen (če), z izjemo
exchange *n.* izmenjava, zamenjava; ~ **office** *n.*
  menjalnica
exciting *adj.* vznemirljiv, razburljiv

excursion *n.* ekskurzija, izlet; **one-day** ~ enodnevni izlet

excuse *n.* opravičilo; *v.* opravičiti (se), oprostiti

exercise *n.* vaja; *v.* vaditi, vežbati

exhibition *n.* razstava

exit *n.* izhod; *v.* oditi (ven)

expect *v.* pričakovati, slutiti

expense *n.* strošek, izdatek

expensive *adj.* drag; **too** ~ predrago

experience *n.* izkušnja, doživetje

experiment *n.* poskus

expert *n.* ekspert, specialist

explain *v.* razložiti, pojasniti

export *n.* izvoz (*bus.*)

express *adj.* hiter, ekspresen

expression *n.* izraz

extend *v.* razširiti, raztegniti

extension *n.* podaljšek

external *adj.* zunanji, eksteren

extinguish *v.* ugasniti, pogasiti

extinguisher *n.* gasilni aparat

extra *adv.* dodatno, posebej

extraordinary *adj.* nenavaden

eye *n.* oko; ~s *n.* oči (*pl.*)

eyebrow *n.* obrv

eyelash *n.* trepalnica

F

face *n.* obraz

fact *n.* dejstvo, ugotovitev

factory *n.* tovarna, delavnica

faculty *n.* fakulteta; **law** ~ *n.* pravna fakulteta

failure *n.* napaka, motnja

faint *v.* onesvestiti se, omedleti

fair *adj.* pošten, jasen; svetel, blond; *n.* sejem

fall *v.* pasti, padati
false *adj.* lažen, ponarejen, varljiv
family *n.* družina, rodbina
famous *adj.* slaven, znan, znamenit
fan *n.* oboževalec, navdušenec
fantasy *n.* fantazija, domišljija
far *adj.* daleč
fare *n.* voznina; ulov
farm *n.* kmetija, posestvo
farmer *n.* kmet, poljedelec
fascism *n.* fašizem
fashion *n.* moda
fast *adj.* hiter
fasten *v.* pritrditi, pripneti; ~ **the seat belt** *v.* pripeti
    varnostni pas
fat *n.* maščoba; *adj.* debel, masten
father *n.* oče, oči (*fam.*); ~**-in-law** *n.* tast
favor *n.* usluga; prednost
favorite *adj.* najljubši, priljubljen
fear *n.* strah, bojazen; *v.* bati se; spoštovati
feast *n.* pojedina, gostija
feature *n.* karakteristika, lastnost, poteza
February *n.* februar
fee *n.* vstopnina, članarina
feed *v.* hraniti, krmiti (*zool.*)
feel *v.* čutiti, občutiti; zaznati
feeling *n.* občutek, čustvo, otip
feet *n.* noge
fence *n.* ograja, plot
fender *n.* blatnik (*autom.*)
ferry *n.* trajekt
fever *n.* vročica, mrzlica
few *adj.* malo, nekaj, nekateri
field *n.* polje, njiva; igrišče
fig *n.* figa
fight *n.* boj, borba, spopad; *v.* boriti se, spopasti se
file *n.* datoteka, kartoteka; vrsta

fill *v.* napolniti, izpolniti
fillet *n.* (ribji) zrezek
filter *n.* filter
finance *n.* finance, kapital
fine *adj.* fin, odličen
finger *n.* prst; **index ~** *n.* kazalec
fir tree *n.* jelka
fire *n.* ogenj; **~place** *n.* ognjišče, kamin; **~wood**
  n.f.pl. drva; **~man** *n.* gasilec
firm *adj.* trden, čvrst; *n.* podjetje, družba, firma
first *num.* prvi
fish *n.* riba; *v.* ribariti
five *num.* pet
fix *v.* popraviti, pripraviti
flag *n.* zastava
flash *n.* blisk, blišč; **~light** *n.* žepna baterija
flat *n.* stanovanje; **three-bedroom ~** *n.* trosobno
  stanovanje
flavor *n.* okus, vonj, aroma; *v.* okusiti, začiniti (*culin.*)
flax *n.* lan
flight *n.* polet, let; **~ attendant** *n.* stevard
floor *n.* nadstropje; tla; **fifth ~** *n.* peto nadstropje
florist *n.* cvetličar
flour *n.* moka, prašek
flower *n.* roža, cvetlica
flu *n.* gripa
flute *n.* flavta
fly *n.* muha; *v.* leteti
fog *n.* megla
folk *n.* ljudje, ljudstvo; **~lore** *n.* folklora, tradicija
follow *v.* slediti
food *n.* hrana, živila
fool *n.* bedak, norec
foot *n.* noga; **~wear** *n.* obutev; **to go on ~** *v.* iti peš
for *prep.* za; zaradi; namesto; **~ him** zanj; **~ good** za
  vedno
forbid *v.* prepovedati

force *n.* sila; *v.* izsiliti, vsiliti

forecast *n.* napoved; **weather** ~ *n.* vremenska napoved

forehead *n.* čelo

foreign *adj.* tuj, zunanji; ~ **exchange** *n.* devize; menjalnica

foreigner *n.* tujec

forename *n.* osebno, krstno ime

forest *n.* gozd

forget *v.* pozabiti

forgive *v.* oprostiti

fork *n.* vilice

form *n.* oblika, forma, obrazec; *v.* oblikovati, ustvariti

former *n.* bivši, prejšnji

fortune *n.* bogastvo

forward *v.* naprej, dalje

fountain *n.* fontana, vodnjak

four *num.* štiri

fox *n.* lisica

frame *n.* okvir, zgradba

franc *n.* frank

frank *adj.* pošten, direkten

free *adj.* svoboden, prost, neoviran; brezplačen

freedom *n.* svoboda

freeze *v.* zmrzniti, zledeneti

freezer *n.* hladilnik

fresco *n.* freska

fresh *adj.* svež, nov; ~ **fruit** *n.* sveže sadje

Friday *n.* petek

fried *adj.* ocvrt; ~ **chicken** *n.* ocvrti piščanec

friend *n.* prijatelj

frog *n.* žaba

from *prep.* od, iz, s/z; ~ **above** od zgoraj; ~ **the beginning** od začetka

frontier *n.* meja

frost *n.* slana, zmrzal; mraz

frozen *adj.* zmrznjen
fruit *n.* sadje
fry *v.* cvreti
fuel *n.* gorivo
fun *adj.* zabaven, smešen; *n.* zabava, šala, razvedrilo; **to have ~** *v.* zabavati se
funeral *n.* pogreb, pokop
funny *adj.* smešen, duhovit
fur *n.* krzno, kožuhovina
furniture *n.* pohištvo; **office ~** *n.* pisarniško pohištvo
future *adj.* prihodnji, bodoči

G

gain *v.* dobiti, zaslužiti, pridobiti
gallery *n.* galerija; **art ~** *n.* umetnostna galerija
gallon *n.* galona
gamble *v.* kockati, igrati na srečo
game *n.* igra, zabava, tekma; divjačina (*culin.*)
garage *n.* garaža
garbage *n.* smeti, odpadki
garden *n.* vrt, nasad
garlic *n.* česen
gas *n.* plin; bencin; **~ stove** *n.* plinski kuhalnik
gas station *n.* bencinska postaja
gasoline *n.* bencin
gather *v.* zbrati se, zbirati
gear *n.* prestava, naprava; **~box** *n.* menjalnik (*autom.*)
general *adj.* splošen, navaden; **~ hospital** *n.* splošna bolnica
gentleman *n.* kavalir, gospod
geography *n.* geografija, zemljepis
geology *n.* geologija
germ *n.* bakterija

get *v.* dobiti, nabaviti; ujeti; razumeti; **to ~ off** *v.*
izstopiti

gift *n.* darilo, sposobnost

ginger *n.* ingver

girl *n.* deklica, dekle, punca

girlfriend *n.* punca

give *v.* dati; **~ back** vrniti; **~ up** odnehati; **~ away**
oddati, dati stran; izdati

glacier *n.* ledenik

glad (to be) *v.* biti vesel

glass *n.* steklo; kozarec; leča

glove *n.* rokavica; **ski ~s** *n.* smučarske rokavice

glue *n.* lepilo

go *v.* iti; oditi

goal *n.* gol, cilj, naloga

goat *n.* koza; **~ cheese** *n.* kozji sir (*culin.*)

god *n.* bog, božanstvo; **thank God!** hvala Bogu!

gold *adj.* zlat; *n.* zlató

golf *n.* golf; **miniature ~** *n.* mini golf (*sp.*)

good *adj.* dober, ljubezniv; obilen; pravi

good-bye *interj.* zbogom, nasvidenje

goose *n.* gos

goulash *n.* golaž (*culin.*)

government *n.* vlada, vodstvo

graduation *n.* matura (high school)

gram *n.* gram

grammar *n.* slovnica, gramatika

gramophone *n.* gramofon

grand *adj.* velik, imeniten

grandchildren *n.* vnuki

granddaughter *n.* vnukinja

grandfather *n.* ded, dedek

grandmother *n.* babica, stara mama

grandparents *n.* stari starši

grandson *n.* vnuk

grape *n.* grozdje

grapefruit *n.* grenivka

grass *n.* trava, pašnik
grateful *adj.* hvaležen
grave *n.* grob
gray *n.* siva, brezbarvna
grease *n.* mazilo, maščoba
great *adj.* velik, precejšen; imeniten, izvrsten
green *n.* zelen; neizkušen
greet *v.* pozdraviti; odgovoriti
greeting *n.* pozdrav, dobrodošlica
grilled *adj.* (pečen) na žaru; ~ **meat** *n.* meso na žaru
  (*culin.*)
grocery *n.* špecerija
ground *n.* dno, tla, zemlja
group *n.* skupina, gruča, množica; **musical** ~ *n.*
  ansambel, glasbena skupina
grow *v.* rasti; ~ **up** *v.* odrasti, zrasti
guarantee *n.* jamstvo, garancija
guard *n.* straža, preža; *v.* stražiti, čuvati
guest *n.* gost; ~**house** *n.* gostišče; ~ **room** *n.* soba za
  goste
guide *n.* vodič, vodnik; ~**book on Central Europe**
  vodič po Srednji Evropi
guilty *adj.* kriv
guitar *n.* kitara; **acoustic** ~ *n.* akustična kitara
gulf *n.* zaliv, tolmin
gun *n.* pištola, puška
gym *n.* telovadba; telovadnica
gymnastics *n.* gimnastika, telovadba
gynecologist *n.* ginekolog
gypsy *n.* cigan

H

hair *n.* las, lasje (*pl.*), dlaka; ~**dresser** *n.* frizer;
  ~**dryer** *n.* sušilec za lase
half *adj.* pol, na pol

hall *n.* avla, hodnik, dvorana
ham *n.* šunka, gnjat; **~-and-cheese sandwich** *n.* sendvič z šunko in sirom
hamburger *n.* hamburger, pleskavica
hammer *n.* kladivo; *v.* zabiti
hand *n.* roka; pomoč; **~bag** *n.* torbica; **~ brake** *n.* ročna zavora
handsome *adj.* lep, postaven
hang *v.* viseti, obesiti
hanger *n.* obešalnik
happen *v.* zgoditi se, pripetiti se
happy *adj.* vesel, srečen, zadovoljen; **~ birthday!** vse najboljše!
harbor *n.* pristan, pristanišče
hard *adj.* trd, težek, težaven; **~ly** *adv.* komaj, s težavo
harm *n.* škoda, krivica; *v.* škoditi
harmonica *n.* harmonika
harvest *n.* letina
hat *n.* klobuk
hatchet *n.* sekira
hate *n.* sovraštvo; *v.* sovražiti
have *v.* imeti; vsebovati
hazelnut *n.* lešnik
he *pron.* on, moški
head *n.* glava; *adj.* glavni; **~ache** *n.* glavobol; **~quarters** *n.* sedež, uprava (*bus.*)
heal *v.* zdraviti, celiti (se)
health *n.* zdravje, zdravstvo; **~ insurance** *n.* zdravstveno zavarovanje
hear *v.* slišati; **I can't ~ well** ne slišim dobro
heart *n.* srce; duša; **~ disease** *n.* bolezen srca; **~ attack** *n.* infarkt
heat *n.* vročica, toplota; *v.* segreti, ogrevati
heating *n.* gretje, kurjava
heavy *adj.* težek, obilen; naporen
hectare *n.* hektar

hedgehog *n.* jež
heel *n.* peta; **high ~s** *n.* visoke pete
heir *n.* dedič, naslednik
helicopter *n.* helikopter
hello *interj.* halo (*tel.*); živjo
helmet *n.* čelada
help *n.* pomoč; *v.* pomagati
hen *n.* kokoš
her *pron.* ona; njej
herb *n.* zelišča; **~al tea** *n.* zeliščni čaj
here *adv.* tukaj, tu, semkaj
hero *n.* heroj
hide *v.* skriti, prikriti
high *adj.* visok, višji; važen; **~ school** *n.* srednja
   šola, gimazija
highway *n.* avtocesta
hike *v.* hoditi, pešačiti
hiking *n.* pešačenje, pohod; izlet
hill *n.* grič, hrib
him *pron.* njega, ga; njemu, mu
hint *n.* namig
his *pron.* njegov
history *n.* zgodovina
hit *v.* udariti, zadeti
hitchhike *v.* štopati
hockey *n.* hokej; **ice ~** *n.* hokej na ledu (*sp.*)
hole *n.* luknja, jama
hold *v.* držati; **~ on** počakajte
holiday *n.* počitnice, praznik
home *adj.* domač, hišen; *n.* dom; **~sickness** *n.*
   domotožje; **~ country** *n.* domovina
homosexual *n.* homoseksualec; *adj.* homoseksualen
honest *adj.* pošten, odkrit, odkritosrčen
honey *n.* med
honeymoon *n.* medeni tedeni
honor *n.* čast, spoštovanje
hood *n.* kapuca

hope *n.* upanje; *v.* upati, nadejati se
hormone *n.* hormon
horn *n.* rog, trobilo (*autom.*)
horrible *adj.* grozen, strašen
horror *n.* groza; ~ **movie** *n.* grozljivka
horse *n.* konj; ~**race** *n.* konjska dirka
horseradish *n.* hren
hospital *n.* bolnica, bolnišnica, klinika
hospitality *n.* gostoljubnost
host *n.* gostitelj; *v.* gostiti
hostel *n.* prenočišče; **youth** ~ mladinsko prenočišče
hot *adj.* vroč; pekoč; razgret, razvnet
hotel *n.* hotel
hour *n.* ura, čas; **working** ~**s** *n.* delovni čas
house *n.* hiša, dom; ~**hold** *n.* gospodinjstvo;
housekeeper *n.* oskrbnca, gospodinja
how *adv.* kako; ~ **many?** koliko?; ~ **much?** koliko?;
~ **are you?** kako si/ste?
huge *adj.* ogromen, silen
human *adj.* človeški; *n.* človek
humanitarian *adj.* humanitaren; ~ **aid** *n.*
humanitarna pomoč
humor *n.* humor
hundred *num.* sto
hungry *adj.* lačen
hunt *n.* lov; *v.* loviti
hurry *v.* hiteti; ~ **up!** *interj.* pohiti!
hurt *adj.* ranjen, poškodovan; *v.* poškodovati, raniti
husband *n.* mož, soprog; **ex-**~ *n.* bivši mož
hut *n.* koliba, koča
hygiene *n.* higiena

I

ice *adj.* leden; *n.* led; ~ **cream** *n.* sladoled; ~ **hockey**
n. hokej na ledu
I.D. *n.* osebna izkaznica

idea *n.* ideja, zamisel
identify *v.* identificirati, prepoznati
identity *n.* identiteta
if *conj.* če, ko
ignition *n.* vžig, zažig (*autom.*)
ill *adj.* bolan, slab
illness *n.* bolezen
illustration *n.* ilustracija, risba
imagination *n.* domišljija, fantazija
immediate *adj.* nenaden, takojšen, neposreden
immigration *n.* imigracija
impolite *adj.* neprijazen, nevljuden
important *adj.* pomemben, važen
impossible *adj.* nemogoč, neverjeten
impression *n.* vtis, dojem, občutek
impressionism *n.* impresionizem
improve *v.* izboljšati, popraviti, izpopolniti
improvise *v.* improvizirati
in *prep.* v, na; *adv.* notri, noter
inch *n.* palec, cola (2. 54 cm)
included *adj.* vključen, vštet; **breakfast** ~ zajtrk
    vštet v ceno
income *n.* dohódek, plača, zaslužek; **monthly** ~
    mesečna plača
incorrect *adj.* nepravilen, nekorekten
increase *v.* (z)večati, povečati
independent *adj.* neodvisen, samostojen
index *n.* kazalo
indicator *n.* kazalec
indigestion *n.* slaba prebava
individual *adj.* individualen, posamezen; *n.*
    posameznik
industry *n.* industrija; **timber** ~ *n.* lesna industrija
inexpensive *adj.* poceni, cenen
infant *n.* dete, dojenček
infection *n.* infekcija, okužba
inflammation *n.* oteklina

influence *n.* vpliv; moč
information *n.* informacija, podatki
inhabitant *n.* prebivalec, stanovalec
injection *n.* injekcija
injury *n.* rana, poškodba
injustice *n.* krivica
ink *n.* črnilo
inland *n.* notranjost (dežele)
inn *n.* gostilna, gostišče
inpatient *adj.* nepotrpežljiv
inquire *v.* poizvedovati, preiskovati
inscription *n.* vpis, napis
insect *n.* insekt, žuželka
inside *n.* notranjost, notranja stran
instant *adj.* takojšen, trenuten; *n.* trenutek
instead *adv.* namesto
institution *n.* inštitut, ustanova
instructions *n.* navodila
instructor *n.* inštruktor, vaditelj
instrument *n.* inštrument
insurance *n.* zavarovanje
intellectual *n.* intelektualec
intelligent *adj.* inteligenten, pameten
intention *n.* namen, namera
interest *n.* interes, zanimanje; obrest; ~ **rate** *n.*
  obrestna mera (*comm.*)
interesting *adj.* zanimiv
interior *adj.* notranji; **Ministry of the Interior** *n.*
  Ministrstvo za notranje zadeve
international *adj.* mednaroden
interpreter *n.* tolmač
interrupt *v.* prekiniti
interview *n.* intervju; *v.* spraševati
intimate *adj.* intimen
into *prep.* v; **to translate ~ English** *v.* prevesti v
  angleščino

introduce *v.* predstaviti, uvesti; **let me ~...** naj vam predstavim...
introduction *n.* uvod, uvajanje
invalid *adj.* neveljaven
invention *n.* izum, iznajdba, najdba
investigation *n.* preiskava, raziskava
invitation *n.* povabilo, vabilo
invoice *n.* račun, faktura
iodine *n.* jod; **tincture of ~** *n.* jodova tinktura
iron *adj.* železen; *n.* železo, likalnik; *v.* likati
is *v.* je (*3rd person*; *to be*)
Islam *n.* Islam
island *n.* otok
issue *n.* izdaja, zadeva; *v.* izdati
Istra *n.* Istra; **Slovene ~** *n.* Slovenska Istra
it *pron.* ono, to (*nt.*)
item *n.* točka, predmet; postavka
itinerary *n.* potovalni načrt, plan
ivy *n.* bršljan

J

jacket *n.* jakna, jopič, suknjič
jam *n.* marmelada; **strawberry ~** *n.* jagodna marmelada
January *n.* januar
jaw *n.* čeljust
jealousy *n.* ljubosumnost
jeans *n.* kavbojke
jeep *n.* džip
jelly *n.* žele, želatina
jerk *n.* idiot, bedak
jersey *n.* pulover
jet *n.* avion, (reaktivno) letalo
Jew *n.* Žid
jewel *n.* dragulj

jewelry *n.* dragulji, nakit
job *n.* služba, delo, opravilo, posel
join *v.* pridružiti se, združiti se; povezati se
joke *n.* šala, vic
journal *n.* dnevnik, časopis, revija
journalist *n.* novinar
journey *n.* potovanje
judge *n.* sodnik; *v.* soditi
jug *n.* vrč, bokal
juice *n.* sok; **orange ~** *n.* pomarančni sok
July *n.* julij
jump *v.* skočiti, poskakovati
jumper *n.* pulover, jopica
June *n.* junij
just *adv.* pravkar, ravno; komaj
justice *n.* pravičnost, pravica; **Court of Justice** *n.* sodišče

K

Karst *n.* Kras
keep *v.* držati, obdržati, ohraniti; **~ up** *v.* nadaljevati
key *n.* ključ; geslo
kidney *n.* ledvica
kill *v.* ubiti, umoriti
kilogram *n.* kilogram
kilometer *n.* kilometer
kind *n.* vrsta, razred, zvrst
king *n.* kralj
kingdom *n.* kraljestvo; **United K~** *n.* Velika Britanija
kiss *v.* poljubiti
kitchen *n.* kuhinja; **~ furniture** *n.* kuhinjsko pohištvo
knapsack *n.* nahrbtnik, oprtnik
knee *n.* koleno

knickers *n.* ženske spodnje hlače
knife *n.* nož, bodalo, rezilo
knob *n.* gumb
knock *v.* trkati, potrkati; udariti, suniti
knot *n.* vozel, pentlja
know *v.* vedeti; znati; poznati; **I ~ her** poznam jo; **I ~ vem**
knowledge *n.* znanje, vednost, poznavanje

L

label *n.* etiketa, nalepka
laboratory *n.* laboratorij
lace *n.* čipka; **Idria ~** *n.* Idrijska čipka
lack *n.* pomanjkanje (nečesa)
ladder *n.* lestev
lady *n.* gospa, dama
lamb *n.* jagnje
land *n.* zemlja, kopno
landlord *n.* hišni lastnik, gospodar
landscape *n.* pokrajina
lane *n.* kolovoz, podeželska cesta
language *n.* jezik; **foreign ~** *n.* tuj jezik
large *adj.* velik, ogromen
late *adj.* pozen, kasen; pokojni
later *adj.* pozneje, kasneje
laugh *v.* smejati se
laundry *n.* pralnica; perilo
lavatory *n.* umivalnica; umivalnik
law *n.* právo; **international ~** *n.* mednarodno pravo
lawn *n.* travnata površina ob hiši
lawyer *n.* odvetnik, pravnik
layer *n.* plast, sloj
lazy *adj.* len
lead *v.* voditi
leaf *n.* list (*bot.*)

learn *v.* (na)učiti se; izvedeti
leather *n.* usnje; ~ **jacket** *n.* usnjena jakna
leave *v.* oditi, zapustiti
lecture *n.* predavanje; branje, čtivo
leek *n.* por
left *n.* leva; ~ **hand** *n.* leva roka; **turn** ~ zavijte levo
leg *n.* noga
legal *adj.* legalen; dovoljen
lemon *n.* limona
lemonade *n.* limonada
lend *v.* posoditi; dati
lenses *n.* leče
lesion *n.* poškodba, rana
lesson *n.* lekcija
letter *n.* črka; pismo; **capital** ~ *n.* velika črka;
    registered ~ *n.* priporočeno pismo
level *n.* stopnja, nivo
library *n.* knjižnica
license *n.* dovoljenje, licenca
lie *v.* ležati, počivati; nahajati se
life *n.* življenje
lift *n.* dvigalo; *v.* dvigniti
light *n.* svetloba, luč; *adj.* svetel
lighter *n.* vžigalnik
like *v.* imeti rad, marati, ugajati
lily *n.* lilija (*bot.*)
limit *n.* meja, skrajnost
linden *n.* lipa (*f.bot.*); lipovec (*m.bot.*)
line *n.* črta, linija, poteza
lion *n.* lev
lip *n.* ustnica, usta
lipstick *n.* šminka
liquid *adj.* tekoč, voden
liquor *n.* alkoholna pijača
list *n.* seznam
listen *v.* poslušati
literature *n.* književnost, literatura

little *adj.* majhen, droben
live *v.* živeti; stanovati
liver *n.* jetra
living room *n.* dnevna soba
lizard *n.* kuščar
load *n.* tovor, breme; **heavy ~** *n.* težek tovor
loaf *n.* štruca; **~ of bread** *n.* štruca kruha
lobster *n.* jastog
local *adj.* krajeven, lokalen; **~ police station** *n.*
　krajevna policijska postaja
lock *n.* zakleniti; **un~** *v.* odkleniti
lodging *n.* stanovanje, nastanitev
loft *n.* podstrešje
lollipop *n.* lizika
long *adj.* dolg; dolgotrajen
look *v.* gledati, ogledovati si; **to ~ for** *v.* iskati
loose *v.* odvezati, razrahljati
loosen *v.* zrahljati, odvezati, razrahljati; *adj.* zrahljan
lose *v.* izgubiti (se)
loud *adj.* glasen
love *n.* ljubezen; *v.* ljubiti (nekoga)
lovely *adj.* prisrčen, ljubek
low *adj.* nizek, majhen
luck *n.* sreča; **good ~!** *interj.* srečno!
luggage *n.* prtljaga
lunch *n.* kosilo, obed
lungs *n.* pljuča
luxurious *adj.* razkošen, luksuzen

M

macaroni *n.* makaroni
machine *n.* aparat, naprava, stroj
mad *adj.* nor, besen, blazen
madame *n.* gospa
magazine *n.* revija

mail *n.* pošta
mailbox *n.* poštni nabiralnik
main *adj.* glaven, bistven; ~ **road** *n.* glavna cesta
maintenance *n.* vzdrževanje
major *adj.* glaven, pomemben
majority *n.* večina
make *v.* narediti, delati, napraviti, izdelovati
male *adj.* moški
manager *n.* upravnik
mandarin *n.* mandarina
many *adv.* mnogo, številni
map *n.* zemljevid, karta; ~ **of Slovenia** *n.* zemljevid
   Slovenije
maple *n.* javor
marble *n.* marmor
March *n.* marec
margarine *n.* margarina
mark *n.* znak, znamenje; *v.* označiti
market *n.* trg, tržišče; ~ **research** *n.* raziskava
   tržišča (*bus.*)
marriage *n.* poroka, zakon
married *adj.* poročen
mass *n.* masa, množica; maša (*relig.*)
massage *n.* masaža
master *n.* gospodar; mojster
material *n.* material, snov
mathematics *n.* matematika
matinee *n.* matineja
mature *adj.* zrel
May *n.* maj
maybe *adv.* mogoče, morda
mayonnaise *n.* majoneza
mayor *n.* župan
meal *n.* obrok, jed
meaning *n.* pomen, namen
measure *n.* mera; *v.* meriti

meat *n.* meso
mechanic *n.* avtomehanik
medal *n.* medalja
medical *adj.* zdravniški; ~ **exam** *n.* zdravniški
   pregled
medicine *n.* medicina
medieval *adj.* srednjeveški
medium *n.* srednji, povprečen
meet *v.* srečati; spoznati
meeting *n.* sestanek; **business** ~ *n.* poslovni
   sestanek
melon *n.* melona; **water~** *n.* lubenica
member *n.* član
membership fee *n.* članarina
memory *n.* spomin
menu *n.* jedilni list, meni
message *n.* sporočilo
metal *n.* kovina
meteorology *n.* meteorologija
meter *n.* meter; **square ~** *n.* kvadratni meter
middle *n.* sredina; *adj.* srednji
midnight *n.* polnoč
migraine *n.* migrena
mile *n.* milja
milk *n.* mleko
mill *n.* mlin; **~er** *n.* mlinar
million *num.* miljon
mind *n.* misel, razum
mineral *adj.* mineralen; ~ **water** *n.* mineralna voda
ministry *n.* ministrstvo
minor *adj.* manjši; mladoleten
minority *n.* manjšina
mint *n.* meta *(bot.)*
minute *n.* minuta
miracle *n.* čudež
mirror *n.* ogledalo, zrcalo

miss *v.* zamuditi, zgrešiti; pogrešati;

Miss (Ms.) Gospodična (gdč.)

mistake *n.* napaka, pomota

misunderstanding *n.* nesporazum

mix *v.* mešati, zmešati

modern *adj.* moderen; sodoben; ~ **art** *n.* moderna umetnost

moist *adj.* vlažen

moisture *n.* vlaga

mole *n.* krt

monastery *n.* samostan

Monday *n.* ponedeljek

money *n.* denar

monk *n.* menih

monkey *n.* opica

month *n.* mesec

monument *n.* spomenik

moon *n.* mesec, luna; **full ~** *n.* polna luna

more *adv.* več, bolj, še

morning *n.* jutro; **good ~!** dobro jutro!

mosque *n.* mošeja (*relig.*)

mosquito *n.* komar

moss *n.* mah

most *adv.* najbolj, naj; **the ~ beautiful** *adj.* najlepši

mother *n.* mati, mama (*fam.*)

mother-in-law *n.* tašča

motor *n.* motor; **~bike** *n.* motorno kolo; **~way** *n.* avtocesta

mountain *n.* gora; ~ **bike** *n.* gorsko kolo

mouse *n.* miš

moustache *n.* brki

mouth *n.* usta

move *v.* premikati se; preseliti se

movie *n.* film

Mr. *n.* gospod (g.)

Mrs. *n.* gospa (ga.)

Ms. *n.* gospodična, gospa (gdč., ga.)
much *adv.* mnogo, zelo, veliko
mud *n.* blato
mulatto *n.* mulat
municipality *n.* občina
murder *n.* umor
muscle *n.* mišica
museum *n.* muzej
mushroom *n.* goba; ~ **soup** *n.* gobova juha
music *n.* glasba, muzika
musician *n.* glasbenik
Muslim *n.* musliman
must *v.* morati
mustard *n.* gorčica
my *pron.* moj
myth *n.* mit

N

nail *n.* noht; žebelj
naked *adj.* gol, nag
name *n.* ime; ~ **day** *n.* god
napkin *n.* prtiček; brisača
narrow *adj.* ozek, tesen
nation *n.* narod; ~al **dish** *adj.* narodna jed
nationality *n.* narodnost
native *n.* domačin; domorodec
NATO *n.* NATO
nature *n.* narava
near *adj.* bližnji; *adv.* blizu
necessary *adj.* potreben, nujen
neck *n.* vrat
necklace *n.* ogrlica, verižica
need *v.* rabiti, potrebovati
needle *n.* igla, brizgalka

neighbor *n.* sosed
nephew *n.* nečak
nervous *adj.* živčen, nervozen
nest *n.* gnezdo
net *n.* mreža
nettle *n.* kopriva (*bot.*)
never *adv.* nikoli
new *adj.* nov; svež
news *n.* novice, vesti; poročila
newspaper *n.* časopis
newsstand *n.* kiosk
next *adj.* naslednji
nice *adj.* lep, fin
niece *n.* nečákinja
night *n.* noč; **~dress** *n.* spalna srajca; **good ~!** lahko noč!
nine *num.* devet
nipple *n.* bradavica
no *adv.* ne; noben
nobody *adv.* nihče
noise *n.* hrup, trušč
none *adv.* nobeden, nihče
noodles *n.* rezanci, testenine
normal *adj.* normalen, navaden
north *n.* sever; **in the ~** *adv.* na severu; **towards the ~** *adv.* na, proti severu
northern *adj.* severni
nose *n.* nos
notary *n.* notar
note *v.* zabeležiti; **~book** *n.* zvezek, beležnica
nothing *adv.* nič
notification *n.* obvestilo
November *n.* november
now *adv.* zdaj, sedaj; torej
number *n.* število, številka
nurse *n.* medicinska sestra
nut *n.* oreh, lešnik

O

object *n.* predmet, stvar
obligatory *adj.* obvezen
occupation *n.* poklic
ocean *n.* ocean; **Atlantic O~** *n.* Atlantski ocean;
    Pacific O~ *n.* Tihi ocean
October *n.* oktober
odd *adj.* čuden, čudaški; neparen
offer *n.* ponudba; *v.* ponuditi
office *n.* pisarna, urad
often *adv.* pogosto
oil *n.* olje; **olive ~** *n.* olivno olje
OK *interj.* prav, v redu
old *adj.* star
olive *n.* oliva
on *prep.* na
once *num.* enkrat
one *num.* ena, en; **~ way street** *n.* enosmerna cesta
onion *n.* čebula
only *adv.* samo, le
open *adj.* odprt, odprto; *v.* odpreti
opera *n.* opera
operation *n.* operacija
opinion *n.* mnenje, misel
opportunity *n.* priložnost, možnost
opposite *adj.* nasproten
optician *n.* optik
or *conj.* ali
orange *n.* oranžna (barva); pomaranča; *adj.* oranžen
orchestra *n.* orkester, band
order *v.* naročiti; *n.* ukaz, naročilo
ordinary *adj.* navaden, vsakdanji
organization *n.* organizacija
origin *n.* izvor, poreklo
original *adj.* originalen, izviren
other *adj.* drug, ostali

ounce *n.* unča (28. 35 gr)
our *pron.* naš
out *adv.* ven, zunaj, izven
oven *n.* pečica, peč; **electric** ~ *n.* električna pečica
over *adv.* čez, preko
own *adj.* lasten, svoj; *v.* imeti
owner *n.* lastnik
oxygen *n.* kisik
oyster *n.* ostriga

P

pack *v.* pakirati
package *n.* paket
pain *n.* bolečina, bol
paint *v.* barvati, slikati; beliti (*constr.*)
paintbrush *n.* čopič
painter *n.* slikar
palace *n.* palača
pale *adj.* bled; svetel
palm *n.* dlan
pancake *n.* palačinka
pants *n.* hlače
paper *n.* papir; listina
pardon *interj.* oprostite
parents *n.* starši; **grand~** *n.* stari starši
park *n.* park, nasad; **~ing lot** *n.* parkiríšče
parliament *n.* parlament
parsley *n.* peteršilj
part *n.* del, kos; **the biggest/smallest** ~ *n.* največji/najmanjši kos
party *n.* zabava; *v.* zabavati se
passenger *n.* potnik
passport *n.* potni list; ~ **number** *n.* številka potnega lista
password *n.* geslo

past *adj.* minuli, pretekli
pasta *n.* testenine
patch *n.* obliž
pâté *n.* pašteta
path *n.* pot, steza
patient *n.* pacient, bolnik
pavement *n.* pločnik
pay *v.* plačati; **~ment** *n.* plačilo
pea *n.* grah
peace *n.* mir, spokojnost
peach *n.* breskev
pear *n.* hruška
pedestrian *n.* pešec
pen *n.* pero
pencil *n.* svinčnik
peninsula *n.* polotok
pension *n.* pension; pokojnina
people *n.* ljudje
pepper *n.* paprika; **red ~** *n.* rdeča paprika
percent *n.* odstotek
performance *n.* nastop, predstava
perfume *n.* parfum, dišava
permission *n.* dovoljenje
person *n.* oseba, posameznik
pet *n.* domača žival (*zool.*)
petanque *n.* balinanje (*sp.*)
petrol *n.* bencin; **~ station** *n.* bencinska postaja
pharmacy *n.* lekarna; **the nearest ~** *n.* najbližja
  lekarna
pheasant *n.* fazan
philology *n.* filologija, jezikoslovje
philosophy *n.* filozofija
phone *n.* telefon; *v.* telefonirati, (po)klicati
photograph *n.* fotografija; slika
phrase *n.* fraza
physics *n.* fizika; **quantum ~** *n.* kvantna fizika
piano *n.* klavir

pick *v.* izbrati, pobrati; prebirati
picnic *n.* piknik
picture *n.* slika, risba
piece *n.* kos, del
pier *n.* pomol
pigeon *n.* golob
pill *n.* tableta
pillow *n.* blazina
pink *n.* roza (barva); *adj.* roza, rozast
place *n.* kraj, prostor, mesto
plan *n.* načrt, plan, projekt
plastic *n.* plastika; *adj.* plastičen
plate *n.* krožnik
play *v.* igrati
player *n.* igralec
playground *n.* igrišče
pleasant *adj.* prijeten, prijazen
please *interj.* prosim
plug *n.* čep; vtikač
plum *n.* sliva
plural *n.* množina
P.M. *adv.* popoldne
pneumonia *n.* pljučnica
pocket *n.* žep; **~knife** *n.* žepni nož
poet *n.* pesnik
poison *n.* strup
police *n.* policija; **~man** *n.* policaj; **~woman** *n.* policistka
polish *n.* lak; **nail ~** *n.* lak za nohte
polite *adj.* prijazen, uglajen
politics *n.* politika
poor *adj.* reven; ubog
poppy *n.* mak
popular *adj.* populiaren, razširjen
pork *n.* svinjina
porridge *n.* kaša
port *n.* pristanišče, luka

portion *n.* del, delež
possible *adj.* možen, mogoč
post *v.* objaviti, naznaniti, poslati; *n.* pošta
postal/zip code *n.* poštna številka
postcard *n.* razglednica
pot *n.* lonec
potato *n.* krompir
poverty *n.* beda, revščina
power *n.* moč, tok; oblast (*admin.*)
Prague *n.* Praga
pray *v.* moliti; ~**er** *n.* molitev
precise *adj.* točen, natančen
precious *n.* dragocen
prefer *v.* imeti rajši, imeti raje
pregnancy *n.* nosečnost
prepare *v.* pripraviti
prescription *n.* recept; predpis
present *n.* darilo
pretty *adj.* lep, čeden
price *n.* cena
priest *n.* duhovnik
prison *n.* zapor
private *adj.* privaten, zaseben
prize *n.* nagrada; **Nobel Prize** *n.* Nobelova nagrada
probably *adv.* verjetno, najbrž
product *n.* izdelek, proizvod; ~**ion** *n.* proizvodnja
profession *n.* poklic; **liberal** ~**s** *n.* svobodni poklici
prohibit *v.* prepovedati
promise *n.* obljuba; *v.* obljubiti
pronunciation *n.* izgovorjava
proof *n.* dokaz
property *n.* posest, lastnina
proposal *n.* predlog, ponudba
protect *v.* zaščititi, varovati
protein *n.* beljakovina
pub *n.* bar, gostilna, točilnica
public *adj.* javen, znan; *n.* javnost

pudding *n.* puding
pull *v.* potegniti, vleči
pullover *n.* pulover
punctual *adj.* točen
puppy *n.* mladič (*zool.*)
purchase *n.* nakup; *v.* kupiti
pure *adj.* čist, jasen
purpose *n.* namen, cilj
push *v.* potisniti, poriniti
put *v.* položiti, postaviti; ~ **down** *v.* odložiti; ~ **up**
   (**with**) *v.* prenašati

Q

qualification *n.* kvalifikacija
quality *n.* kvaliteta
quantity *n.* količina
quarter *n.* četrt, četrtina
queen *n.* kraljica
question *n.* vprašanje
questionnaire *n.* vprašalnik
queue *n.* vrsta; *v.* stati v vrsti
quick *adj.* hiter, uren, nagel
quiet *adj.* tih, miren
quit *v.* prenehati, (o)pustiti
quite *adv.* kar, dokaj; ~ **well** *interj.* kar dobro

R

rabbit *n.* zajec
race *n.* tekma, dirka; rasa
racket *n.* lopar; **tennis** ~ *n.* teniški lopar
radio *n.* radio
radish *n.* redkev; **horse~** *n.* hren
rail *n.* tir, tračnica

railway *n.* železnica, kolodvor
rain *n.* dež
rainbow *n.* mavrica
raincoat *n.* dežni plašč
rare *adj.* nenavaden, redek
raspberry *n.* malina
rate *n.* tarifa, cena; ritem, tempo
raw *adj.* surov
razor *n.* britvica
read *v.* brati, čitati; razbrati
ready *adj.* pripravljen, gotov
real *adj.* resničen, realen
reason *n.* razlog, vzrok
receipt *n.* račun
receive *v.* (s)prejeti
receiver *n.* prejemnik
reception *n.* recepcija
recipe *n.* (kuhinjski) recept
record *n.* rekord; plošča; ~ **player** *n.* gramofon
recreation *n.* rekreacija, razvedrilo
red *n.* rdeča (barva); *adj.* rdeč
refrigerator *n.* hladilnik
refugee *n.* begunec, ubežnik
region *n.* regija
register *v.* registrirati, vpisati; ~**ed letter** *n.* priporočeno pismo
regular *adj.* navaden, reden, normalen
relation *n.* odnos, razmerje; ~**ship** *n.* zveza
relatives *n.* sorodstvo
relax *v.* sprostiti se
religion *n.* vera, religija
remain *v.* ostati
remains *n.* ostanki
remember *v.* spomniti se, zapomniti se
renaissance *n.* renesanca
renew *v.* obnoviti; renovirati (*constr.*)
rent *v.* najeti; dati v najem; *n.* najemnina
repair *v.* popraviti

repeat *v.* ponoviti
request *n.* zahteva; *v.* zahtevati
research *n.* raziskava; *v.* raziskovati
reservation *n.* rezervacija
residence *n.* bivališče, rezidenca
resort *n.* letovišče
responsibility *n.* odgovornost
responsible *adj.* odgovoren
rest *v.* počivati
restaurant *n.* restavracija, gostilna
result *n.* rezultat, izid
retired *adj.* upokojen
return *v.* vrniti (se)
reward *n.* nagrada; *v.* nagraditi
rib *n.* rebrce
rice *n.* riž
rich *adj.* bogat, premožen
ride *v.* jahati, jezditi
right *n.* desno; ~ **hand** *n.* desnica
ring *n.* prstan; obroč, krog; *v.* pozvoniti; **wedding ~**
  n. poročni prstan
river *n.* reka
road *n.* cesta, pot; **main ~** *n.* glavna cesta
rob *v.* ropati, krasti
rock *n.* skala; čer (*mar.*)
rodent *n.* glodalec (*zool.*)
Rome *n.* Rim
roof *n.* streha, krov
room *n.* soba, prostor; **living ~** *n.* dnevna soba
root *n.* korenina
rope *n.* vrv
rose *n.* vrtnica (*bot.*)
rotten *adj.* gnil, pokvarjen
row *n.* vrsta, niz, kolona
royal *adj.* kraljevi, kraljevski
rubber *n.* guma; radirka
rubbish *n.* odpadki, smeti

rucksack *n.* nahrbtnik
rule *n.* pravilo, predpis
rum *n.* rum
run *v.* teči, drveti, pobegniti
rural *adj.* kmečki; ~ /(**countryside**) **tourism** *n.*
kmečki turizem

S

sad *adj.* žalosten, otožen
safe *adj.* varen, siguren, zanesljiv
safety *n.* varnost; ~ **belt** *n.* varnostni pas
sail *v.* jadrati; ~**boat** *n.* jadrnica
sailor *n.* mornar
salad *n.* solata; **fruit** ~ *n.* sadna solata
salary *n.* plača, zaslužek, dohodek
sale *n.* prodaja
sales *n.* razprodaja; ~**man** *n.* prodajalec; ~**woman** *n.*
prodajalka
salmon *n.* losos
salt *n.* sol; *v.* soliti
salve *n.* mazilo
same *adj.* isti, enak
sand *n.* pesek
sandwich *n.* sendvič
satisfied *adj.* zadovoljen
Saturday *n.* sobota
sauce *n.* omaka, sok; ~**pan** *n.* ponev
sauerkraut *n.* kislo zelje (*culin.*)
sausage *n.* klobasa; **Carniolan** ~ *n.* Kranjska
klobasa
save *v.* rešiti, shraniti; zaščititi
saxophone *n.* saksofon
say *v.* reči, izjaviti, govoriti
scarf *n.* šal
scent *n.* duh, vonj, dišava; aroma

schedule *n.* urnik, tabela, seznam
scholarship *n.* štipendija
school *n.* šola; **elementary** ~ *n.* osnovna šola
science *n.* znanost, veda; **social** ~ *n.* družbena veda
scientific *adj.* znanstven
scientist *n.* znanstvenik
scissors *n.* škarje
score *n.* točka; rezultat
scream *n.* krik, vrisk; *v.* kričati, vpiti
screen *n.* zaslon, ekran
screwdriver *n.* odvijač
sculptor *n.* kipar
sculpture *n.* kip
sea *n.* morje; **~sickness** *n.* morska bolezen
seagull *n.* galeb
search *n.* iskanje; *v.* iskati, preiskovati
seaside *n.* morska obala, morski breg
season *n.* letni čas, sezona; **high** ~ *n.* visoka sezona
seat *n.* sedež, stol; ~ **belt** *n.* varnostni pas
seaweed *n.* alga
second *n.* sekunda; *adj.* second; **~-rate** *adj.*
   drugorazreden
secret *n.* skrivnost, tajnost
secretary *n.* tajnik, tajnica
secure *adj.* varen, zanesljiv; *v.* zavarovati
see *v.* videti, zagledati, opaziti
seek *v.* iskati
select *v.* izbrati
self-service *n.* samopostrežba
sell *v.* prodajati, trgovati
send *v.* poslati, odposlati
sender *n.* pošiljatelj
sense *n.* čut, čutilo; občutek
sensitive *adj.* občutljiv
sentence *n.* stavek
separate *adj.* ločen
September *n.* september

serious *adj.* resen, resnoben
serve *v.* služiti, servirati
service *n.* storitev, služba
set *n.* postaviti, namestiti, naravnati
seven *num.* sedem
sew *v.* šivati
shadow *n.* senca, hlad
shake *v.* tresti, stresti; zavhiteti
shame *n.* sramota, sram
shampoo *n.* šampon
shape *n.* oblika, forma, lik
share *n.* delež; *v.* deliti, porazdeliti
shark *n.* morski pes
sharp *adj.* oster, špičast
shave *v.* obriti, briti
she *pron.* ona
sheep *n.* ovca; **~dog** *n.* ovčar
sheet *n.* rjuha; list
shelf *n.* polica
shelter *n.* zavetišče
shine *n.* lesk, sij, sijaj; *v.* sijati, svetiti (se)
ship *n.* ladja, barka
shirt *n.* srajca; **T-~** *n.* majica (s kratkimi rokavi)
shock *n.* šok
shoe *n.* čevelj; **~laces** *n.* vezalke; **~maker** *n.* čevljar
shop *n.* trgovina, prodajalna; **~ assistant** *n.*
    prodajalec, prodajalka
shore *n.* obala, kopno
short *adj.* kratek, majhen, nizek; **~cut** *n.* bližnjica
show *n.* predstava; *v.* razkazovati, kazati, voditi
shower *n.* prha; *v.* prhati se
shut *v.* zapreti; **~ the window!** zapri okno!
shy *adj.* plašen, boječ, sramežljiv
sick *adj.* bolan
side *n.* stran, bok
sidewalk *n.* pločnik
sign *n.* znak, znamenje; *v.* označiti, podpisati

signature *n.* podpis
silence *n.* tišina, mir, molk
silk *n.* svila
silver *n.* srebro; *adj.* srebrn
similar *adj.* podoben
simple *adj.* preprost, enostaven
since *adv.* odkar, od; ~ **yesterday** *adv.* od včeraj
sincere *adj.* pošten, odkrit
sing *v.* peti, prepevati
single *adj.* samski
singular *n.* ednina (*gram.*)
sink *n.* umivalnik; *v.* potoniti, potopiti (se)
sister *n.* sestra; ~ **-in-law** *n.* svakinja
sit *v.* sedeti; ~ **down** *n.* usesti se
situation *n.* situacija, položaj, stanje
six *num.* šest
size *n.* velikost, debelina, dimenzija
skate *v.* drsati, kotalkati
skating rink *n.* drsališče
ski *n.* smučanje; *v.* smučati
skill *n.* veščina, spretnost, sposobnost
skin *n.* koža; lupina (*bot.*)
skirt *n.* krilo
sky *n.* nebo
skyscraper *n.* nebotičnik
sledge *n.* sani, sanke
sleep *v.* spati; ~**ing bag** *n.* spalna vreča
sleepy *adv.* zaspan, dremav
sleeve *n.* rokav; **long/short** ~ *n.* dolg/kratek rokav
slice *n.* kos, rezina
slippers *n.* copati
Slovene *adj.* slovenski (*m.*), slovenska (*f.*);
  ~ **language** *n.* slovenščina
Slovenia *n.* Slovenija
slow *adj.* počasen
small *adj.* majhen, neznaten
smart *adj.* pameten, bister

smell *n.* vonj, duh; *v.* duhati, zavohati
smile *n.* nasmeh; *v.* nasmehniti se
smoke *n.* dim; *v.* kaditi; **no smoking!** kaditi
   prepovedano!
smoker *n.* kadilec
smooth *adj.* gladek, raven
snack *n.* prigrizek; **~ bar** *n.* okrepčevalnica, bife
snail *n.* polž
snake *n.* kača
sneeze *v.* kihati
snow *n.* sneg; *v.* snežiti, zasnežiti
soap *n.* milo
sober *adj.* trezen; **~ up** *n.* strezniti se
soccer *n.* nogomet
social *adj.* družaben, družben; **~ism** *n.* socializem
society *n.* družba, skupnost
socks *n.* nogavice
sofa *n.* kavč, divan
soft *adj.* mehek, blag
soil *n.* zemlja, prst, gruda
soldier *n.* vojak, borec
solid *adj.* trden, čvrst
some *adv.* nekoliko, nekaj, neki, en, kakršenkoli;
   ~ apples nekaj jabolk
somebody *adv.* nekdo
something *adv.* nekaj
sometimes *adv.* včasih
son *n.* sin
son-in-law *n.* zet
song *n.* pesem
soon *adv.* kmalu, v kratkem
sore *adj.* boleč; ranjen; **~ throat** *n.* boleče grlo
soul *n.* duša, duh
sound *n.* zvok, glas, šum
soup *n.* juha; **beef ~** *n.* goveja juha
sour *adj.* kisel
source *n.* izvir, poreklo

south *n.* jug; **in the ~** *adv.* na jugu; **towards the ~** *adv.* proti jugu

southern *adj.* južni

souvenir *n.* spominek

spa *n.* toplice, zdravilišče

space *n.* prostor; vesolje

spare *adj.* nadomesten, rezerven; **~ part** *n.* nadomestni del

spark *n.* iskra; **~plug** *n.* svečka (*autom.*)

speak *v.* govoriti

speaker *n.* govornik; zvočnik

special *adj.* poseben, nenavaden

specialty *n.* posebnost, specialiteta

species *n.* vrsta, rasa

speech *n.* govor, nagovor

speed *n.* hitrost; naglica; **~ometer** *n.* brzinometer, števec hitrosti (*autom.*)

spell *v.* črkovati

spend *v.* zapraviti, porabiti, potrošiti

spice *n.* začimba, dišava

spider *n.* pajek

spinach *n.* špinača

spine *n.* hrbtenica; hrbet

spoon *n.* žlica; **tea~** *n.* (čajna) žlička

sport *n.* šport

spot *n.* mesto, pika, lisa

spring *n.* pomlad; vzmet (*tec.*)

square *n.* kvadrat; **~ meter** *n.* kvadratni meter

stable *n.* hlev

stadium *n.* (športni) stadion

stage *n.* oder; faza

stain *n.* madež

stairs *n.* stopnice

stalactite *n.* kapnik, stalaktit

stamp *n.* znamka; kolek (*admin.*); **rubber ~** *n.* žig, pečat

stand *n.* stati; ~ **up** *v.* vstati
star *n.* zvezda
start *v.* začeti, povzročiti, pričeti
state *n.* država; stanje; *adj.* državen
statement *n.* izjava
station *n.* postaja; **bus** ~ *n.* avtobusna postaja
statue *n.* kip
stay *v.* ostati, prebivati
steak *n.* zrezek; **beef~** *n.* biftek (*culin.*)
steal *v.* (u)krasti
steel *n.* jeklo; **stainless** ~ *n.* nerjaveče jeklo (*constr.*)
stepdaughter *n.* pastorka
stepfather *n.* očim
stepmother *n.* mačeha
stepson *n.* pastorek
stick *n.* palica; *v.* prilepiti
still *adv.* miren, nepremičen, negiben
stink *v.* smrdeti, zaudarjati
stock *n.* delnica; ~ **market** *n.* (delniška) borza
stomach *n.* trebuh
stone *n.* kamen
stop *v.* (za)ustaviti, prekiniti, prenehati
storm *n.* nevihta, vihár, neurje
story *n.* zgodba, pripovedka, bajka
stove *n.* peč, štedilnik
straight *adv.* naravnost, ravno
strange *adj.* čuden, tuj, nepoznan
straps *n.* naramnice
strawberry *n.* jagoda
stream *n.* tok, struja (*comp.*); potok
street *n.* cesta, ulica
strength *n.* moč, jakost, sila
string *n.* vrvica, žica, struna
stroke *n.* kap
strong *adj.* močen, krepak
study *v.* študirati (*univ.*); učiti se, proučevati

stuffed *adj.* polnjen, napolnjen; ~ **peppers** *n.* polnjene paprike (*culin.*)

subscription *n.* naročnina, abonma

suburb *n.* predmestje, mestna okolica

subway *n.* podzemna železnica; (zemeljski) podhod

success *n.* uspeh; **~ful** *adj.* uspešen

sudden *adv.* nenaden, nepričakovan

sugar *n.* sladkor; **brown** ~ *n.* rjavi sladkor

suit *n.* obleka; **law~** *n.* tožba (*law*); **~case** *n.* kovček, avtovka

suite *n.* apartma

summer *n.* poletje

sun *n.* sonce; **~bathe** *v.* sončiti se; **sun rise/set** *n.* sončni vzhod/zahod

Sunday *n.* nedelja

supermarket *n.* supermarket, veleblagovnica

supper *n.* večerja

supreme *adj.* najvišji, vrhovni; **S~ Court** *n.* vrhovno sodišče

sure *adj.* gotov, zanesljiv, varen

surface *n.* površina, površje

surgeon *n.* kirurg

surgery *n.* operacija

surname *n.* priimek

surprise *n.* presenečenje, začudenje

swallow *v.* pogoltniti; *n.* lastovica (*zool.*)

swamp *n.* močvirje

swan *n.* labod

sweat *n.* pot, znoj; *v.* znojiti se, potiti se

sweater *n.* pulover

sweet *adj.* sladek; ljubezniv

swim *v.* plavati; **~mer** *n.* plavalec; **~ming pool** *n.* bazen

swimsuit *n.* kopalke

switch *n.* stikalo; **switch on/off** *v.* prižgati/ugasniti

syringe *n.* brizgalka, injekcija

syrup *n.* sirup

system *n.* sistem, sestav

T

table *n.* miza; **~cloth** *n.* prt
tail *n.* rep
tailor *n.* krojač
take *v.* vzeti, prijeti; **~ away** *v.* odvzeti; **~ care** *n.*
   paziti (na)
tale *n.* pripovedka; basen (about animals)
talk *v.* govoriti, pogovarjati se
tall *adj.* visok
tape *n.* kaseta; **~ recorder** *n.* magnetofon; **adhesive**
   ~ *n.* samolepilni trak
task *n.* naloga, opravilo
taste *n.* okus; *v.* (p)okusiti
tavern *n.* taverna
tax *n.* davek, taksa; **V.A.T.** *n.* davek na dodano
   vrednost (DDV) (*admin.*)
taxi *n.* taksi; **~ rank** *n.* vrsta taksijev
tea *n.* čaj; **~pot** *n.* čajnik
teach *v.* učiti, poučeváti
teacher *n.* učitelj
team *n.* ekipa, moštvo
tears *n.* solze
technician *n.* tehnik
technology *n.* tehnologija
teenager *n.* najstnik
telegram *n.* telegram
telephone *n.* telefon
telescope *n.* daljnogled
television *n.* televizija; **~ program** *n.* televizijski
   program
tell *v.* povedati, reči; sporočiti; razlikovati
temperature *n.* temperatura
ten *num.* deset
tension *n.* napetost
tent *n.* šotor
terrace *n.* terasa

terrible *adj.* strašen, grozen
territory *n.* ozemlje, teritorij
test *n.* test, preizkus, poskus
textbook *n.* učbenik
textile *n.* tkanina, tekstil
than *conj.* kot, kakor; **more** ~ več kot
thank you *interj.* hvala
thanks *n.* zahvala
that *pron.* to; *conj.* da; **so** ~ da bi
theater *n.* gledališče
then *adv.* nato, potem; takrat
there *adv.* tam, tamkaj, tu
thermometer *n.* termometer
thick *adj.* debel, grob
thief *n.* lopov, tat
thin *adj.* suh, vitek
thing *n.* stvar, reč, predmet
think *v.* misliti, premišljevati
third *num.* tretji
thirsty *adj.* žejen
this *pron.* ta, to; ~ **time** *adv.* tokrat
thought *n.* misel, ideja
thousand *num.* tisoč
three *num.* tri
through *adv.* skozi, preko, čez
throw *v.* vreči, metati; ~ **up** *v.* bruhati
thunder *n.* grom, grmenje
Thursday *n.* četrtek
tick *n.* klop (*zool.*)
ticket *n.* karta, listek, vstopnica; **parking** ~ *n.*
  parkirni listek
tidy *adj.* čist, snažen, urejen
tie *n.* kravata; *v.* zavezati, zavozlati
tight *adj.* tesen
time *n.* čas; ~**table** *n.* urnik
tin *n.* pločevinka, konserva; ~ **opener** *n.* odpirač
tip *n.* napitnina; *v.* dati napitnino

tired *adj.* utrujen

tissue *n.* robček; ~ **paper** *n.* papirnati robček

to *prep.* k, proti, do, v, na, poleg; ~ **Miami** v Miami

toast *n.* popečen kruh (*culin.*); zdravica

today *adv.* danes

together *adv.* skupaj, skupno

toilet *n.* stranišče, kopalnica

token *n.* žeton; znak

toll *n.* cestnína, pristojbina (*trans.*)

tomato *n.* paradižnik

tomorrow *adv.* jutri; **the day after** ~ *adv.* pojutrišnjem

ton *n.* tona

tone *n.* ton, zvok, glas

tongs *n.* klešče

tongue *n.* jezik; **mother** ~ *n.* materinščina

tonight *adv.* danes zvečer, nocoj

too *adv.* tudi; preveč, odveč

tools *n.* orodje

tooth *n.* zob; **~ache** *n.* zobobol; **~pick** *n.* zobotrebec; **~brush** *n.* zobna ščetka

top *n.* vrh, vrhunec; na vrhu; konica

torch *n.* bakla

total *n.* cel, ves, skupen

touch *n.* dotik; *v.* dotikati se, otipati

tour *n.* izlet, tura

tourism *n.* turizem

tourist *n.* turist, izletnik

towards *adv.* k, proti, v smeri

towel *n.* brisača

tower *n.* stolp

town *n.* kraj, mesto

toxic *adj.* strupen

toy *n.* igrača; ~ **shop** *n.* trgovina z igračami

track *n.* steza, pot

trade *n.* trgovina; **~mark** *n.* zaščitni znak

tradition *n.* tradicija, izročilo
traffic *n.* promet, trgovanje; **air** ~ *n.* zračni promet
trailer *n.* prikolica
train *n.* vlak; *v.* vzgajati, izšolati
translator *n.* prevajalec, prevajalka
transmission *n.* menjalnik (*autom.*)
transport *n.* prevoz, transport
travel *v.* potovati; ~ **agency** *n.* potovalna agencija
traveler *n.* potnik
tree *n.* drevo
triangle *n.* trikotnik
trip *n.* potovanje, izlet
trolley *n.* voziček; tramvaj
trouble *n.* težava, problem, neprijetnost
trousers *n.* hlače
trout *n.* postrv; **Soča** ~ *n.* Soška postrv
truck *n.* kamion, tovornjak
true *adj.* resničen, pravi
trunk *n.* prtljažnik; deblo, steblo (*bot.*)
trust *n.* zaupanje; *v.* zaupati
truth *n.* resnica, resničnost
try *v.* poskusiti, preizkusiti
tsar *n.* car
T-shirt *n.* majica (s kratkimi rokavi)
tub *n.* kad, banja
tube *n.* cev, cevka, kanal
Tuesday *n.* torek
tunnel *n.* tunel
turn *v.* zaviti, obrniti, spremeniti (smer); ~ **on/off** *v.*
   prižgati/ugasniti
turtle *n.* želva
TV *n.* televizija
twenty *num.* dvajset
twice *num.* dvakrat
twin *n.* dvojček, dvojčica
two *num.* dva, dve

U

ugly *adj.* grd
umbrella *n.* dežnik
uncle *n.* stric
unconscious *adj.* nezavesten
under *adv.* pod, spodaj
underwear *n.* spodnje perilo
unemployed *n., adj.* nezaposlen, brezposelen
uniform *n.* uniforma
union *n.* zveza, združenje
unit *n.* enota, kos
universe *n.* vesolje, kozmos
university *n.* univerza
unknown *adj.* nepoznan, neznan
unless *adv.* razen če
unlock *v.* odkleniti
until *adv.* do, vse do
unusual *adj.* nenavaden, izreden
up *adv.* gor, zgoraj, navzgor
upper *adj.* (z)gornji, višji
up-to-date *adv.* moderen, sodoben
urgent *adj.* nujen
use *v.* uporabljati, rabiti, koristiti; **~ful** *adj.*
    uporaben, koristen
user *n.* uporabnik, potrošnik
usual *adj.* običajen, navaden

V

vacant *adj.* prazen, nezaseden, prost
vacation *n.* počitnice, oddih
vaccinate *v.* cepiti
vacuum cleaner *n.* sesalnik
valid *adj.* veljaven, utemeljen
valley *n.* dolina
van *n.* kombi

vegetable *n.* zelenjava
vegetarian *n.* vegetarijanec, vegetarijanka
vehicle *n.* vozilo, voz
vein *n.* vena, žila
velvet *n.* žamet
Venice *n.* Benetke; ~ **Carnival** *n.* Beneški karneval
verb *n.* glagol; **irregular** ~ *n.* nepravilni glagol
verify *v.* preveriti, potrditi
version *n.* različica
very *adv.* zelo, zares; ~ **well** prav
vest *n.* telovnik
victory *n.* zmaga, uspeh
Vienna *n.* Dunaj; **Viennese waltz** *n.* Dunajski valček
view *n.* razgled; *v.* gledati; **~er** *n.* gledalec, opazovalec
village *n.* vas, majhen kraj
vinegar *n.* kis
vineyard *n.* vinograd
violet *n.* vijolična (barva); *adj.* vijoličen
violin *n.* violina
viper *n.* modras
visa *n.* vizum; **multiple-entry** ~ *n.* vizum za večkratni vstop
visit *n.* obisk; *v.* obiskati; **~or** *n.* obiskovalec, gost
vitamin *n.* vitamin
vocabulary *n.* besedni zaklad
voice *n.* glas, zvok
volleyball *n.* odbojka
voltage *n.* napetost električnega toka
volume *n.* jakost (zvoka), glasnost; knjiga, zvezek
vomit *v.* bruhati

W

wage *n.* plača, zaslužek
wagon *n.* vagon
waist *n.* pas, opasje; **~coat** *n.* telovnik, brezrokavnik

wait (for) *v.* čakati, počakati (na)
waiter *n.* natakar
waiting room *n.* čakalnica
waitress *n.* natakarica
wake up *v.* zbuditi (se), prebuditi (se)
walk *n.* hod, hoja, pešačenje; *v.* hoditi, pešačiti
wall *n.* stena, zid
wallet *n.* denarnica, listnica
walnut *n.* oreh
want *v.* hoteti, želeti
war *n.* vojna, boj
wardrobe *n.* garderoba
warehouse *n.* skladišče
warm *adj.* topel, ogret, vroč
warning *n.* opozorilo, svarilo
wash *v.* prati, umivati; **~ing machine** *n.* pralni stroj
wasp *n.* osa
watch *v.* gledati, opazovati
water *n.* voda; vodovje
waterfall *n.* slap, kaskada
waterproof *adj.* nepremočljiv
watermelon *n.* lubenica
wax *n.* vosek
way *n.* pot, cesta, steza, proga; **~ in/out** *n.* vhod/izhod
WC *n.* stranišče
we *pron.* mi
weak *adj.* šibek, slaboten
weapon *n.* orožje
wear *v.* nositi, imeti na sebi
weather *n.* vreme; **bad ~** *n.* slabo vreme
wedding *n.* poroka, svatba
Wednesday *n.* sreda
week *n.* teden; **~day** *n.* delavnik; **~end** *n.* konec
   tedna, vikend
weigh *v.* tehtati
weight *n.* teža
welcome *n.* dobrodošlica; *interj.* dobrodošli
well *adv.* dobro, primerno, pravilno

west *n.* zahôd; **in the** ~ *adv.* na zahodu; **towards the** ~ *adv.* proti zahodu
western *adj.* zahoden
wet *adj.* moker, premočen
whale *n.* kit
what *pron.* kaj, koliko; ~ **for?** zakaj?; **about** ~ **?** o čem?
wheat *n.* pšenica
wheel *n.* kolo, kolesje; krmilo (*autom.*)
wheelchair *n.* invalidski voziček
when *conj.* ko, kadar
where *conj.* kje, kam, kod
whether *conj.* ali, če; ~ **you like it or not** če ti je prav ali ne
which *pron.* kateri, katera
while *adv.* medtem; trenutek, hip, čas
whiskey *n.* viski
white *n.* bela (barva); *adj.* bel; ~ **person** *n.* belec
who *pron.* kdo, koga; tisti, tista
whole *adj.* cel, celoten, ves; ~**sale** *n.* prodaja na debelo
why *conj.* zakaj, čemu, zaradi česa
wide *adj.* širen, širok, obsežen
widow *n.* vdova; ~**er** *n.* vdovec
width *n.* širina
wife *n.* žena, soproga
wig *n.* lasulja
wild *adj.* divji, neukročen
will *n.* volja, želja
win *v.* zmagati, pridobiti
wind *n.* veter; vihar; ~**shield** *n.* vetrobran (*autom.*)
window *n.* okno
wine *n.* vino; ~ **cellar** *n.* vinska klet
wing *n.* krilo
winter *n.* zima
wire *n.* žica, kabel; ~**less** *adj.* brezžičen
wise *adj.* moder
wish *v.* želja, voščilo; *v.* želeti, voščiti, hoteti

with *conj.* z, s; **with you** s tabo
without *adv.* brez; ~ **a doubt** brez dvoma
witness *n.* priča; *v.* pričati, prisostvovati
woman *n.* ženska, žena
wonderful *adj.* čudovit, krasen
wood *n.* les; **~en furniture** *n.* leseno pohištvo
wool *n.* vôlna; volnen; **~en blanket** *n.* volnena odeja
word *n.* beseda
work *n.* delo, posel, opravilo, služba; ~ **day** *n.*
    delavnik; **~shop** *n.* delavnica
worker *n.* delavec
world *n.* svet, Zemlja
worm *n.* črv
worry *n.* skrb, vznemirjenje; *v.* skrbeti; **don't**
    worry! ne skrbi!
worse *adj.* huje, hujši, slabše
worst *adj.* najhujši
wound *n.* rana, poškodba; *v.* raniti, poškodovati
wrap *v.* zaviti, omotati
wrist *n.* zapestje; **~watch** *n.* zapestna ura
write *v.* (na)pisati, zapisati
writer *n.* pisatelj, pisec
writing desk *n.* pisalna miza
wrong *adj.* napačen, nepravi, naroben

X

X-mas (Christmas) *n.* Božič
X ray *n.* rentgen

Y

yacht *n.* jahta
yard *n.* jard (0.914m); dvorišče
year *n.* leto; starost; **I am 30 years old** star-a sem
    trideset let

yeast *n.* kvas (*culin.*)
yellow *n.* rumena (barva); *adj.* rumen
yes *adv.* da, ja
yesterday *adv.* včeraj; ~ **morning** *adv.* včeraj zjutraj
yet *adv.* še vedno, še; doslej, že
yogurt *n.* jogurt
you *pron.* ti, vi, vas; tebe; **I will call you** te
    pokličem.
young *adj.* mlad, nov
your *pron.* tvoj, vaš
youth *n.* mladost, mladina

Z

zebra *n.* zebra; ~ **crossing** *n.* prehod za pešce
    (*trans.*)
zero *n.* nič, nula
zip code *n.* poštna številka
zipper *n.* zadrga
zone *n.* cona, področje, del
zoo *n.* živalski vrt

Phrasebook Contents

Basics

Greetings – Saying Good-bye –
Question Words –
Introductions – Communication Problems

Yes.
Ja./Da.

No.
Ne.

Maybe.
Mogoče.

Thank you.
Hvala.

Please.
Prosim.

You're welcome.
Prosim.

Greetings
(Pozdravljanje)

Hello.
Živjo/Zdravo.

Good morning.
Dobro jutro.

Good afternoon.
Dober dan.

Good evening.
Dober večer.

Welcome.
Dobrodošli.

How are you?
Kako ste? (*pl./sing. form.*)
Kako si? (*sing. fam.*)

Fine.
Dobro.

Okay.
V redu.

So-so.
Tako tako.

Bad.
Slabo.

Don't ask.
Ne vprašaj.

Saying Good-bye
(Poslavljanje)

Bye/Good-bye.
Adijo./Čao.

Until next time.
Nasvidenje.

See you.
Se vidimo.

Good night.
Lahko noč.

Have a nice time!
Lepo se imejte! (*form.*)
Lepo se imej! (*sing. fam.*)

Oh, I am sorry.   Excuse me, (please)...
Oprostite.   **Oprostite, (prosim)...**

Note: Slovenes divide the day into four periods:
morning (6 A.M.–10 A.M.), daytime (11 A.M.–6 P.M.),
evening (6 P.M.–11 P.M.), and night (after 11 P.M.).

Question Words
(**Vprašalnice**)

Where?
Kje?

When?
Kdaj?

What?
Kaj?

How?
Kako?

Who?
Kdo?

Why?
Zakaj?

How? (description)
Kakšen?

Whose?
Čigav?

Which?
Kateri?

Introductions
(**Predstavljanje**)

The polite form of addressing people always takes the same grammatical form as the second person plural. You would use this form for new acquaintances, people of higher status, or elderly people.

to introduce **predstaviti**
to know* **poznati**
to meet **spoznati**

*Learn more about the verb "to know" in the Grammar section.

Do you know Ana? (*pl./sing. form.*)
Poznate Ano?

Do you know Ana? (*sing. fam.*)
Poznaš Ano?

I would like to introduce you to Mrs. Hočevar.
Želim vam predstaviti gospo Hočevar.

Do you know Mr. Novak?
Ali poznate gospoda Novaka?

I am David Smith.
Jaz sem David Smith.

And this is Miss Alice Jackson.
In to je gospodična Alice Jackson.

Nice/glad to meet you.
Me veseli.

What is your name?
Kako vam je ime? (*pl./sing. form.*)
Kako ti je ime? (*sing. fam.*)

Where are you from?
Odkod prihajate? (*pl./sing. form.*)
Odkod si? (*sing. fam.*)

I am from Arizona.
Prihajam iz Arizone.

Communication Problems
(Komunikacijske težave)

I am learning Slovene.
Učim se slovensko.

I don't understand Slovene.
Ne razumem slovensko.

Do you speak English?
Ali govorite angleško?

Would you repeat that, please?
Ali lahko ponovite, prosim?

Would you speak slowly please?
Ali lahko govorite bolj počasi, prosim?

How do you say that in Slovene?
Kako se to reče po slovensko?

Would you write that down, please?
Ali lahko to napišete, prosim?

Would you spell that, please?
Ali lahko to črkujete, prosim?

Travel & Transportation

Bicycle – Taxi – Bus – Train –
Boat – Air Transport – Customs –
Car – Travel Agents

Where?
Kje?

From where?
Odkod?

How far is it?
Kako daleč je?

In which direction is…?
V kateri smeri je…?

Excuse me, how do I get to the bus station?
Oprostite, kako se pride do avtobusne postaje?

I am looking for Pregel street.
Iščem Preglovo ulico.

Excuse me, where is the British embassy?
Oprostite, kje se nahaja Angleška embasada?

I am going to Koper. Which way must I go?
Grem v Koper. V kateri smeri je?

back	**nazaj**
close	**blizu**
down	**dol**
far	**daleč**
left	**levo**

right	**desno**
straight ahead	**naravnost/naprej**
up	**gor**

You may hear...

Turn left at the corner.
Zavijte levo na vogalu.

Turn right after the first light.
Pri prvem semaforju zavijte desno.

Go straight ahead until the end of the street.
Pojdite naravnost do konca ulice.

Cross the bridge and ask again.
Prečkajte most in ponovno vprašajte.

You must turn back and go to the main crossroad.
Pojdite nazaj na glavno križišče.

It's not far.
Ni daleč.

It's quite near.
Je kar blizu.

Bicycle
(**Kolo**)

Traveling by bicycle is common and one of the most efficient forms of transportation in Slovenia. You can find numerous bike routes in the larger cities. Bicycling is permitted on all roads except motorways.

bicycle	**kolo**
bicycle route	**kolesarska steza**
helmet	**zaščitna čelada**
mountain bike	**gorsko kolo**
tire pump	**pumpa**

I would like to rent a bicycle (with all the equipment).
Rad(a) bi najel(a) kolo (z vso opremo).

How much does one hour/all day cost?
Koliko stane ena ura/cel dan?

Taxi
(Taksi)

You can call for a taxi (*taksi*) by phone or you can find one on the street. Cabs can usually be found in front of bus and train terminals as well as on busier city streets. If you are going to stay in the same place for a few days, keep the cabdriver's business card handy. The fare will be less expensive if you always use the same driver. If you are planning to use a credit card, you must say so in advance.

Where's a taxi stand?
Kje je postajališče taksijev?

Are you free?
Ste prosti?

I need a taxi at Dunajska 135.
Potrebujem taksi na Dunajsko cesto 135.

I am in a hurry, so please send it over as soon as possible.
Mudi se mi, zato vas prosim, da ga pošljete čim hitreje.

It should be a rather big car, as we have a lot of
   luggage.
Naj bo večji avto, ker imamo veliko prtljage.

What is the daily rate?
Kakšna je vaša dnevna tarifa?

What is the rate per kilometer?
Kakšna je vaša tarifa za kilometer?

Take me to the airport/train station, please.
Peljite na letališče/železniško postajo.

Please, take me to Tovarniška street.
Peljite, prosim, na Tovarniško ulico.

May I smoke?
Lahko kadim?

Would you please turn on/off the radio?
Lahko, prosim, prižgete/ugasnete radijo?

Please, stop here.   Please, wait.
Ustavite tukaj, prosim.   Prosim, počakajte me.

I shall get out here.
Tukaj izstopim.

May I pay with a credit card/euros?
Lahko plačam s kreditno kartico/z euri?

How much do I owe you?
Koliko je?

May I have the receipt, please?
Ali lahko, prosim, dobim račun?

May I have your business card, please?
Lahko dobim vašo vizitko, prosim?

Bus
(Avtobus)

bus	avtobus
bus station	avtobusna postaja
bus stop	avtobusno postajališče
bus token	žeton za avtobus
ticket	vozovnica, vozna karta
baggage ticket	prtljažni listek
one-way ticket	enosmerna vozovnica
return ticket	povratna vozovnica

Where is the nearest bus stop?
Kje je najbližja avtobusna postaja?

Which bus goes to the city center/airport?
Kateri avtobus vozi v center mesta/na letališče?

Does this bus go to the city center?
Ali gre ta avtobus v center mesta?

Please tell me where to get off.
Prosim, povejte mi, kdaj naj izstopim.

I would like to purchase a …
Rad(a) bi kupil(a) …

a one-way ticket to Koper, please.
enosmerno vozovnico za Koper, prosim.

two return tickets to Bled.
dve povratni karti za Bled.

an open ticket for Venice.
odprto karto za Benetke.

Train
(**Vlak**)

arrival	**prihod**
boarding	**vkrcanje**
cancelled	**odpovedan**
delay	**zamuda**
departure	**odhod**
on time	**pravočasno**
platform	**tir**
sleeper	**spalnik**
timetable	**urnik**
train	**vlak**
train station	**železniška postaja**

Where's the ticket office?
Kje je blagajna?

Where can I buy tickets?
Kje lahko kupim karto?

What time does the train leave/arrive?
Kdaj je odhod/prihod vlaka?

Is there an express train to Vienna?
Obstaja direktni vlak za Dunaj?

Does the train have any sleepers?
Ima ta vlak kakšen spalni vagon?

What platform does it leave from?
Iz katerega perona je odhod?

From platform number 5.
Iz perona številka 5.

Do I have to change trains?
Ali moram prestopati?

Is this seat taken/free?
Je ta sedež zaseden/prost?

Where is the restaurant car?
Kje je restavracija?

Boat
(Plovilo)

boat	**čoln**
dock	**privez**
ferry	**trajekt**
hydroplane	**hidrogliser**
sailboat	**jadrnica**
ship	**ladja**

What is the docking fee for a 19ft/39ft sailboat?
Kakšna je cena za privez 6m/12m jadrnice?

Air Transport
(Zračni promet)

airplane	**letalo**
airport	**letališče**
flight	**polet**

flight attendant	**stevard** (*m.*), **stevardesa** (*f.*)
international flights	**mednarodni poleti**
terminal	**terminal**

Where is the terminal for international departures?
Kje je terminal za mednarodne polete?

The flight is delayed for one hour.
Ta let ima eno uro zamude.

This flight has been cancelled.
Ta let je bil odpovedan.

What time does the plane take off?
Kdaj je odhod letala?

The plane takes off at 9:30.
Odhod letala je ob 9:30.

What time are we landing?
Kdaj je pristanek?

Are there any window seats available?
Je ob oknu še kakšen prost sedež?

Is it a direct flight?
Je let direkten?

No, you change flights in Milan.
Ne, prestopate v Milanu.

Is vegetarian food being served on the plane?
Ali na letalu strežejo vegetarijansko hrano?

I am vegetarian.
Sem vegetarijanec(ka).

Is there a duty-free shop at the airport?
Je na letališču kakšna brezcarinska prodajalna?

How much time before boarding begins?
Koliko časa je še do vkrcanja?

I´d like to cancel my reservation.
Rad(a) bi preklical(a) mojo rezervacijo.

I missed the flight for London. When is the next
    departure?
**Zamudil(a) sem odhod letala v London. Kdaj je
    naslednji let?**

The next plane for London is leaving tomorrow at
    11 A.M.
**Naslednji let v London je jutri ob enajstih
    zjutraj.**

Would you like to make a reservation?
Bi radi naredili rezervacijo?

What about transfer flights?
Kaj pa nedirektni leti?

Lost Luggage
(Izgubljena prtljaga)

My luggage has been lost/stolen.
Moja prtljaga je izgubljena/ukradena.

Could you please check it? I arrived from Paris on
    flight number 4657.
**Ali lahko prosim preverite? Prihajam iz Pariza,
    let številka 4657.**

Please notify me if there is something new; I will
be staying in hotel Lev.
**Obvestite me prosim, ko bo kaj novega;
nastanil(a) se bom v hotelu Lev.**

Customs
(Na carini)

Your passport, please.
Potni list, prosim.

How long are you planning to stay in Slovenia?
Kako dolgo nameravate ostati v Sloveniji?

One week/one month.
En teden/en mesec.

Are you traveling together?
Potujete skupaj?

I'm traveling alone.
Potujem sam(a).

I am a citizen of (the) United States/Canada/
United Kingdom/Australia.
**Sem državljan(ka) Združenih držav/Kanade/
Velike Britanije/Avstralije.**

I'm a tourist.　　　　I'm on a business trip.
Sem turist(ka).　　Sem na poslovnem obisku.

I have a transit/entry/multiple entry visa.
Imam prehodni/vhodni/vizum za večkratni vstop.

Have you got anything to declare?
Imate kaj za prijaviti?

I have only personal items/souvenirs/presents.
Imam le osebne reči/spominke/darila.

Which is your luggage?
Katera je vaša prtljaga?

Open it, please.   Is this yours?
Odprite, prosim.   Je to vaše?

What duties do I have to pay?
Kakšno takso moram plačati?

Where are you staying?
Kje boste stanovali?

We're staying in the Hotel Union.
V hotelu Union.

At a friend's place.
Pri prijateljih.

We are going to Hungary/Croatia.
Gremo na Madžarsko/Hrvaško.

Car
(Avto)

Traveling by car in Slovenia is quite safe and relatively easy. While Slovenian drivers do not tend to be as aggressive as some other Europeans, one should be aware that Slovenian streets are much narrower than most American roads, and that you must (almost) always yield the right-of-way to bicyclists.

The speed limit in Slovenia is 50 km (30 mi)/h in towns and villages, 90 km (55 mi)/h on ordinary roads, and 130 km (80 mi)/h on motorways. Seat belts are required and car lights must be turned on at all times.

crossing	**prehod za pešče, zebra**
highway	**avtocesta**
lights	**semafor**
pavement	**pločnik**
street	**cesta**
toll	**cestnina**
tunnel	**tunel, predor**

Be sure to obtain a parking permit (from a street vendor or a newspaper stand) and place it on the dashboard. If you are unsure about the legality of parking on a particular street, ask the locals. Below are some of the traffic restrictions that you should know:

No Parking.
Prepovedano parkiranje.

Delivery only.
Za dostavo.

Parking available/full.
Parkirišče prosto/zasedeno.

Residents only.
Za stanovalce.

At the Gas Station
(Na bencinski črpalki)

Most gas stations are self-service, although older ones still offer full service. (The staff fills the tank for you.)

Fill it up, please.   diesel   gas, petrol
Polno, prosim.   **dizel**   **bencin**

3000 SIT (tolarjev) worth of gas, please.
Natočite za 3000 tolarjev, prosim.

Where can I fill up my tires?
Kje lahko napihnem gume?

I'd like to pay for pump number 9.
Plačam številko 9.

Do you have a map of Slovenia?
Imate zemljevid Slovenije?

Car Trouble
(Težave z avtom)

If you are experiencing car trouble, you should have no difficulty finding a mechanic (**mehanik**) or a tow truck (**pajek**).

I ran out of gas.
Zmanjkalo mi je bencina.

The car won't start.
Avto ne vžge.

TRAVEL & TRANSPORTATION

My front tire is flat.
Sprednja guma je prazna.

Where's the nearest service station?
Kje je najbližja popravljalnica avtomobilov?

Can you fix it?
Lahko odpravite težavo?

I am having a   **Imam težave s/z...**
problem with...

   the battery   **akumulatorjem**
   the brakes   **zavorami**
   the carburetor   **uplinjačem**
   the clutch   **sklopko**
   starting the engine **vžigom**
   the transmission   **menjalnikom**

Can you change...?   **Lahko zamenjate...?**

   the brake fluid   **zavorno tekočino**
   the oil   **motorno olje**
   the tire   **gumo**

Is there a car wash available?
Je tukaj avtopralnica?

How long will it take?
Kako dolgo traja?

How much will it cost?
Koliko stane?

Car Rental
(Izposoja avtomobila)

Car rental agencies are common in Slovenia. Be prepared to show your passport, a valid driver's license, and a credit card.

diesel car	**dizel avto**
family car	**družinski avto**
sports car	**športni avto**
van	**kombi**

I´d like to rent a car.
Rad(a) bi najel(a) avto.

Could you show me the models and prices, please?
Lahko vidim modele in cenik, prosim?

Does the price include mileage/gas?
Ali cena vključuje kilometrino/gorivo?

I want full insurance.
Želim kompletno zavarovanje.

How far is the nearest gas station?
Kako blizu je najbližja bencinska črpalka?

Do you have any road maps?
Imate kakšen zemljevid cest?

What's the speed limit for motorways?
Kakšna je hitrostna omejitev na avtocesti?

Police
(Policija)

fine	**kazen**
police station	**policijska postaja**
speed limit	**hitrostna omejitev**

Your driver's license and car documents
(registration and insurance), please.
**Vozniško (dovoljenje) in dokumente
(registracija in zavarovanje), prosim.**

Somebody has stolen my car/my wallet.
Ukradli so mi avto/denarnico.

Travel Agents
(V turistični agenciji)

Slovenian travel agents offer a wide variety of orga-
nized trips, particularly in Slovenia and the surrounding areas.

I need an (open) plane ticket for New York.
Potrebujem (odprte) avionske karte za New York.

Is there a direct flight to Munich?
Je kakšen direktni let za Muenchen?

Do you organize trips to Pohorje?
Ali organizirate izlete na Pohorje?

We want to spend a week in a seaside hotel.
Radi bi preživeli teden dni v obmorskem hotelu.

We'd like to rent an apartment for a week.
Radi bi najeli stanovanje za en teden.

May I have more information about that hotel?
Ali lahko dobim več podatkov o hotelu?

May I have a brochure?
Imate kakšen prospekt?

Is the camping site in a quiet area?
Se kamping nahaja v mirnem okolju?

What's the weather like this season?
Kakšno je vreme v tem letnem času?

Do I have to pay a deposit to make the reservation?
Ali moramo rezervacijo potrditi z delnim plačilom?

When are we leaving?
Kdaj je odhod?

Do you know where we could find a guest
house/walking tour?
**Ali mogoče veste, kje lahko najdem
gostišče/planinski izlet?**

Is there a discount for children (under 14)?
**Obstaja kakšen popust za otroke (mlajše od
štirinajstih let)?**

Accommodations

How to Make a Reservation –
Check In & Check Out –
Requests – Complaints

Guest houses and camping are very popular with tourists. Guest houses offer an intimate, cozy atmosphere and authentic, home-cooked Slovene cuisine, while camping allows you to experience Slovenia's unspoiled wilderness. Either experience is a must.

bungalow	**bungalov**
camping	**kamp**
guesthouse	**penzion**
hotel	**hotel**
rural hotel	**kmečki turizem**
youth hostel	**mladinski dom**

Excuse me, is there lodging/a hotel nearby?
Oprostite, je tukaj v bližini kakšen hotel/kakšno prenočišče?

Can you recommend to us a pleasant guest house that offers local cuisine?
Nam lahko priporočite prijetno gostišče z dobro hrano?

How to Make a Reservation
(Kako rezervirati prenočišče)

I would like to book two single rooms/one double room.
Rad(a) bi rezerviral(a) dve enoposteljni sobi/eno dvoposteljno sobo.

ACCOMMODATIONS

breakfast included	**z zajtrkom**
full board	**polni penzion**
room service	**sobna strežba**
satellite TV	**satelitska televizija**
with balcony	**z balkonom**
with bath	**z banjo**

What is the price per night?
Koliko stane nočitev?

Do you rent shared rooms?
Ali oddajate postelje v deljenih sobah?

We will arrive next Tuesday.
Prispeli bomo naslednji torek.

We shall stay for a week.
Ostali bom en teden.

Do you accept pets?
So domače živali dovoljene?

The name is Brown.
Na ime Brown.

Would you please confirm the reservation?
Ali lahko, prosim, potrdite rezervacijo?

Is wheelchair access provided?
Ali je možen dostop z invalidskim vozičkom?

Is there handicapped parking?
Imate urejeno parkirišče za dostop invalidnih voznikov?

Check In & Check Out
(Prihod in Odhod)

I booked a room under the name of...
Imam rezervacijo za prenočišče na ime...

We would like a campsite for a tent, a car, and
three people.
Želimo prostor za en šotor, en avto in tri osebe.

Do you have a room for the night?
Ali imate proste sobe?

May I see the room?
Lahko vidim sobo?

Do you have any information about cultural events
or sightseeing tours?
**Ali posredujete informacije o kulturnih
dogodkih in ogledih znamenitosti?**

I am a student.
Sem študent.

This is my student ID.
To je moja študentska izkaznica.

You may hear...

No, we are full.
Ne, vse je zasedeno.

Yes, we do. Would you like a room with one or two
beds?
**Da, imamo sobe. Želite enoposteljno ali
dvoposteljno?**

With a bath or shower only?
Z banjo ali tušem?

For how many nights?
Za koliko noči?

Would you like a campsite close to the bathroom
facilities?
Želite kampirati v bližini sanitarnih objektov?

Long-Term Rentals/Sales

Check the local newspaper (section: **nepremičninski
oglasi**) or a real estate agency (**nepremičninska
agencija**) for long-term rentals and property for sale.

House/Apartment for Rent outside of Ljubljana.
Oddam hišo/stanovanje v bližini Ljubljane.

Studio in Koper for Sale.
Garsonjero v Kopru prodam.

Two Bedroom Apartment for Rent in Ptuj.
Furnished, with cable TV.
**Oddam dvosobno stanovanje na Ptuju;
opremljeno, z kabelsko televizijo.**

Requests
(**Zahteve**)

fresh towels	**sveže brisače**
full board	**polni penzion**
half board	**polpenzion**
hairdryer	**sušilec za lase**

hot water	**topla voda**
laundry	**pralnica**
minibar	**minibar**
room service	**sobna strežba**
safe	**sef**

Where may I park my car?
Kje lahko parkiram avto?

Is there cable/a TV in the room?
Je v sobi televizija/kabelska antena?

When is breakfast/lunch/dinner served?
Kdaj strežete zajtrk/kosilo/večerjo?

Would you tell me where the swimming pool is,
please?
**Mi lahko, prosim, poveste, kje je kakšno
kopališče?**

May I have a room with a balcony/a view of the
mountains?
**Ali lahko dobim sobo z balkonom/z razgledom
na gore?**

May I have the key to room number...?
Ali lahko dobim ključ sobe številka...?

Are there any messages for me?
Imate kakšno sporočilo zame?

Would you please prepare the bill?
Ali lahko pripravite račun?

May I have the brochure for your hotel, please?
Lahko dobim vaš prospekt, please?

ACCOMMODATIONS

Complaints
(Pritožbe)

The room service wasn't good.
Sobna strežba ni bila ravno najboljša.

I request a discount.
Zahtevam popust.

I am bothered by the noise from the street.
Moti me hrup, ki se sliši iz ceste.

I would like to change rooms.
Želim zamenjati sobo.

It says here that children only pay half-price.
**Tukaj piše, da otroci plačajo le polovično
   vstopnino.**

Food & Drink

Table Service – Breakfast – Snacks – Appetizers –
Main Courses – Desserts – Beverages –
Home Delivery – Recipes – At the Market

The wide range of dishes in Slovenian cuisine
clearly reflects the country's varied past. While
many dishes originated in the Republic of Slovenia,
others come from nearby countries and outside cultures. Authentic Slovene food is largely flour-based
(wheat and buckwheat flour) and can be found at
guest houses (*gostilnas*) and Slovenian restaurants.
You'll find the menu (*jedilni list*) changes significantly as you pass from the northeast to the coastal
regions of Slovenia, where saltwater fish are the
local specialty. One should also make sure to take
advantage of the different types of bread that can be
found in Slovenia (white, black, half-black, corn
flour, with seeds, and so on). Tips are not expected
in Slovenia, but you may leave one if the service is
to your liking.

bar	**bar**
buffet/bistro	**bife/bistro**
coffeehouse	**kavarna**
guest house	**gostilna**
pastry shop	**slaščičarna**
pizzeria	**pizzeria, picerija**
restaurant	**restavracija**
snack bar	**okrepčevalnica**
breakfast	**zajtrk**
cold appetizers	**hladne predjedi**
desserts	**sladice**
dishes prepared to order	**jedi po naročilu**

fish	ribe
ready-to-serve dishes	pripravljene jedi
salads	solate
side dishes	prikuhe
snacks	malica
soups	juhe
vegetables	zelenjava
warm appetizers	tople predjedi

Table Service
(Strežba)

Below is a list of common phrases used when ordering a meal.

May we have the menu, please?
Lahko dobimo jedilni list, prosim?

What do you recommend?
Kaj priporočate?

What is the house specialty?
Kaj je vaša hišna specialiteta?

What do you want/What will you have?
Kaj želite/boste?

I don't eat meat; I am allergic/a vegetarian.
**Ne jem mesa. Sem vegeterijanec(ka)/
    alergičen(na).**

I will have beef soup and the two of them will
    have prosciuto with melon.
**Jaz bom govejo juho, onadva pa pršut z
    melono.**

What would you like for…? **Kaj pa…?**

a drink	**za piti**
the main dish	**glavna jed**
the salad	**solata**
dessert	**sladica**

Would you please **Ali lahko prosim**
    bring me…?   **prinesete še…?**

a bottle of wine	**eno steklenico vina**
another plate	**en krožnik**
more bread	**malo kruha**
some ice	**malo ledu**
water	**vodo**

Is/Was everything all right?
Je vse/bilo v redu?

Would you like something else?
Želite še kaj?

The food was cold/stale/bad.
Hrana je bila mrzla/stara/slaba.

It was very good.
Bilo je zelo dobro.

The food is delicious/tasty.
Hrana je odlična/izvrstna/okusna.

May we please have a highchair?
Oprostite, ali imate kakšen otroški stolček?

I would like to pay.
Lahko plačam.

The check, please.
Račun, prosim.

Separate checks, please.
Računajte posebej.

Do you accept credit cards?
Sprejemate kreditne kartice?

I think the check is wrong.
Mislim, da račun ni čisto v redu.

Keep the change.
Obdržite drobiž.

May I have an ashtray, please?
Ali lahko, prosim, prinesete pepelnik?

Where's the restroom, please?
Kje je stranišče?

Breakfast
(**Zajtrk**)

Breakfast is normally included with your room fee. If you are going out, try a nearby *hotel*, *kavarna*, or *slaščičarna*.

I would like to have breakfast for two, please.
Zajtrk za dva, prosim.

Which room are you staying in?
Iz katere sobe ste?

In room number 14.
Iz sobe številka 14.

The breakfast is self-service/served between 7 and
   10 A.M.
**Zajtrk je samopostrežen/se streže od sedmih do
   desetih.**

bread	**kruh**
bread rolls	**žemlje**
toast	**toast/popečeni kruh**
butter	**maslo**
cereal	**kosmiči**
cheese	**sir**
chocolate spread	**čokoladni namaz**
cocoa	**kakav**
coffee*	**kava**
cold/warm milk	**hladno/toplo mleko**
croissant	**rogljiček**
doughnut	**krof**
scrambled eggs	**umešana jajca**
soft-boiled eggs	**mehko kuhano jajce**
eggs sunny-side-up	**jajca na oko**
eggs with ham	**jajca z šunko/slanino**
(fresh) orange juice	**(svež) pomarančni sok**
ham	**šunka**
honey	**med**
jam	**marmelada**
sandwich	**sendvič**
tea	**čaj**
tea with lemon	**čaj z limono**
yogurt	**jogurt**

*For more information on ordering coffee see the
   "Beverages" section.

Snacks
(Malica)

Snacks are served throughout the day. Common snacks include:

burek*	**burek**
Carnelian sausage	**kranjska klobasa**
chestnut	**kostanj**
French fries	**pomfrit**
fried cheese	**pohan sir**
hamburger	**hamburger, pleskavica v lepinji**
ham sandwich	**sendvič z šunko**
dry ham sandwich	**sendvič z pršutom**
hot dog	**hrenovka**
pizza slice	**kos pice**

*Burek, made of flour and different fillings such as meat, apple or cheese, is a very popular, traditional Balkan dish.

four seasons	**štirje letni časi**
ham and cheese	**šunka in sir**
pizza	**pica**
one pizza	**eno pico**
two pizzas	**dve pici**
three pizzas	**tri pice**
seafood	**morski sadeži**
Trieste sauce	**tržaška omaka**

Appetizers
(Predjedi)

Soup is the most common appetizer. *Goveja juha* is a delicious beef soup normally served with noodles.

Kraški pršut (slices of dried ham), *narezek* (home-made salami, smoked meats, cheeses, and pickles), and the following appetizers are frequently served.

beef broth (with noodles)	**goveja juha (z rezanci)**
chicken broth	**kokošja juha**
gravy soup	**obara**
home-cured ham	**domača šunka s**
with horseradish	**hrenom**
kidney bean soup	**fižolova juha**
leek soup	**porova juha**
mushroom soup	**gobova juha**
steak tartar	**tatarski biftek**
vegetable soup	**zelenjavna juha**

Main Courses
(Glavna jed)

Meat

Meat (*meso*), especially pork, chicken and beef, is an important ingredient in Slovene cuisine. Deer and horse meat can be found in many *gostilnas* and most of the butcheries. Do not leave Slovenia without trying one of its many meat stews.

beef cutlet	**naravni zrezek**
beef steak	**biftek**
stuffed bell pepper	**polnjena paprika**
bratwurst	**pečenica**
breaded cutlet with cheese	**ljubljanski zrezek**
cabbage rolls with	**sarma**
diced meat	
chicken	**piščanec**
duck	**raca**

stewed game	**dušena divjačina**
goose	**gos**
grilled meat	**meso na žaru**
spicy grilled meatballs	**čevapčiči**
pork cutlet	**svinjski zrezek**
pork roast	**svinjska pečenka/ zarebrnica**
roasted/fried/ breaded chicken	**pečen/ocvrt/ pohan piščanec**
(blood) sausage	**krvavica**
shish kebob	**ražnjiči**
turkey	**puran**
veal cutlet	**telečji zrezek**

Fish

In the coastal and mountainous regions of Slovenia, you are likely to find delicious fish (*ribe*). Trout (*postrv*), especially the Soča trout (*soška postrv*), is an authentic Slovene speciality.

cattle-fish	**sipa**
crayfish	**rak**
hake fillet	**osličev file**
mussels/clams	**školjke**
oysters	**ostrige**
sardines	**sardele**
scampi	**škampi**
squid	**kalamari/lignji**
tuna	**tuna**
marinated	**v marinadi**
pan-fried à la Trieste	**na tržaški način**

Stew

Stews are very popular, especially during the winter.

barley stew with ribs	**ričet**
beef soup	**goveja juha**
chicken or beef stew	**paprikaš**
chicken or veal soup	**obara**
goulash	**golaž**
sauerkraut stew	**jota**
Serbian bean stew	**pasulj**
tripe	**vampi**

Side dishes

Potatoes (*krompir*) is a common side dish found in Slovene meals, but you can also choose between a variety of flour-based dishes such as *žganci* (groats), *štruklji* (cheese dumplings) or *kruhovi cmoki* (bread dumplings).

buckwheat/corn groats	**ajdovi/koruzni žganci**
french fries	**pomfrit**
hashed brown potatoes	**pražen krompir**
mashed potatoes	**pire krompir**
noodles	**rezanci**
risotto	**rižota**
pasta	**testenine/mlinci**
potato dumplings	**krompirjevi cmoki**
stuffed potatoes	**krompir v oblicah**
with cracklings	**z ocvirki**

Salads

Salad (*solata*) is normally eaten with the main dish and not as an appetizer. The most common salad is composed of lettuce, oil, vinegar and fresh vegetables.

corn salad	**motovilec**
kidney bean salad	**fižolova solata**
lettuce	**zelena solata**
mixed salad	**mešana solata**
potato salad	**krompirjeva solata**
radicchio	**radič**
red beets	**rdeča pesa**
shredded cabbage salad	**zeljnata solata**
string beans salad	**stročji fižol v solati**
tomato salad	**paradižnikova solata**

Fruit and Vegetables

Fresh fruit (*sadje*) and vegetables (*zelenjava*) are available at local markets and supermarkets.

apple	**jabolka**
banana	**banana**
cherry	**češnja**
orange	**pomaranča**
pear	**hruška**
plum	**sliva**

(string) beans	**(stročji) fižol**
broccoli	**brokoli**
brussels sprouts	**brstični ohrovt**
cabbage	**zelje**
carrot	**korenje**

cauliflower	**cvetača**
cucumber	**kumara**
eggplant	**jajčevec, malancane**
garlic	**česen**
mushroom	**gobe**
onion	**čebula**
red/green pepper	**rdeča/zelena paprika**
sauerkraut	**kislo zelje**
sour/sweet turnip	**kisla/sladka repa**
spinach	**špinača**
squash	**bučke**
sweet peas	**grah**
tomato	**paradižnik**

Desserts
(Posladek)

Traditional Slovene cake is called *potica*. Baked from raised rolled dough, it may contain walnuts, raisins, or other fillings. Other popular desserts are *štrudel* (strudel) and *palačinke* (crepes, served with jam or nuts and covered with chocolate).

The *slaščičarna* (pastry shop) or *kavarna* (coffeeshop) are undoubtedly the best places to have a coffee or a pastry. They are normally open all day and you can try such delicious national desserts as:

apple/cheese strudel	**jabolčni/sirov zavitek**
applesauce	**čežana**
Bled cake*	**kremšnita**
cheese-rolled dumplings	**sirovi štruklji**
chocolate/	**čokoladni/**
vanilla ice cream	**vanilijev sladoled**

*Bled cake or kremsnita consists of thin crispy dough, eggs, milk, vanilla scented sugar and whipped cream.

FOOD & DRINK

custard pastry	**kremne rezine/ kremšnite**
deep fried pastry**	**flancati**
fruit with whipped cream	**sadna kupa**
molded cake with raisins	**šarkelj**
omelet with whipped cream and fruit	**pohorska omleta**
prekmurje cake***	**prekmurska gibanica**
raised doughnuts	**krofi**
sweet rolls	**buhteljni**
walnut/tarragon cake	**orehova/ pehtranova potica**

**Flancati are common during Mardi Gras.
***This cake with poppy seeds, curd cheese, walnuts and apples is a national speciality of Slovenia.

Beverages
(Pijače)

Wine is a mainstay of Slovene culture and most Slovenes drink it every day with meals. You can choose between wines from the coastal areas (**teran, refošk, kabernet,** and **merlot**), Štajerska (**rizling, traminec, sauvignon**) or Dolenjska (**cviček**). If you happen to be in Ljubljana during the summer, you can visit the International Wine Fair and taste a variety of local and foreign wines. In November, a festival of new wines is held each year during the Feast of St. Martin. When it comes to beer, there are two national brands, **Union** and **Laško pivo,** that compete with imports. Coffee is normally served after lunch.

bottled beer	**v steklenico**
dark beer	**temno pivo**
draft beer/on tap	**točeno pivo**
apple brandy	**sadjevec**
cherry brandy	**češnjevec**
juniper brandy	**brinjevec**
plum brandy	**slivovka**
William pear brandy	**Viljamovka**
wine brandy	**vinjak**
cognac	**konjak**
apricot juice	**marelični sok**
blueberry juice	**borovničev sok**
orange juice	**pomarančni sok**
peach juice	**breskov sok**
strawberry juice	**jagodni sok**
lemonade	**limonada**
liqueur	**liker**
mineral water	**mineralna voda**
tonic water	**tonik**
whiskey (on the rocks)	**whisky (z ledom)**
fine wine	**buteljčno vino**
house wine	**domače vino**
sparkling wine	**peneče vino**
table wine	**namizno vino**
vintage wine	**arhivsko vino**

Coffee and Tea

In public places, the most commonly served coffee is espresso, while at home people normally prepare traditional Turkish coffee (*turška kava*).

One coffee...	**Eno kavo...**
with milk	**z mlekom**
with whipped cream	**s smetano**

One...   Eno...

   black coffee   **črno kavo**
   cafe au laît   **belo kavo**
   cappuccino   **en kapučino**
   decaffeinated coffee   **kavo brez kafeina**
   double coffee   **dvojno kavo**
   iced coffee   **ledeno kavo**

One...   En...

   chamomile tea   **kamilice**
   herbal tea   **zeliščni čaj**
   mountain tea   **planinski čaj**

Home Delivery
(Dostava na dom)

Hello. We would like to order two large pizzas.
Dober dan. Radi bi naročili dve veliki pici.

One small pizza and a beer please.
Eno majhno pico in pivo, prosim.

The address is Celovška 112.
Naslov je Celovška 112.

How much will it be?
Koliko je to?

How long will it take?
Koliko časa bo trajalo?

Are you paying in cash or with a credit card?
Plačate z gotovino ali s kartico?

With cash/a credit card.
Z gotovino/s kartico.

Recipes
(Recepti)

Slovene ingredients are measured in metric units. Here are some of the most frequently used measurements:

1 dl = ⅓ cup
1 g = 0.35 oz.
250° C = 480°F
225° C = 435°F
190° C = 375°F
175° C = 345°F

one coffee spoon
ena kavna žlička

a glass of warm water
kozarec tople vode

peel/cut in slices/cook
olupite/narežite/skuhajte

fill/fry/flour
napolnite/ocvrite/pomokajte

cinnamon	**cimet**
oil	**olje**
oregano	**origano**
parsley	**peteršilj**
pepper	**poper**
salt	**sol**
sugar	**sladkor**
vinegar	**kis**

Would you please give me the recipe for this dish?
Ali mi lahko date recept za to jed?

blender	**mešalec**
fork	**vilice**
glass	**kozarec**
knife	**nož**
plate	**krožnik**
pot	**lonec**
saucepan	**ponev**
shot glass	**kozarček**
tablespoon	**žlica**
teaspoon	**žlička**

At the Market
(Na tržnici)

Would you please give me...?
Ali mi lahko, prosim, date...?

one kilogram of apples/bread
en kilogram jabolk/kruha

two liters of milk
dva litra mleka

50 decagrams of cheese/ham
50 dekagramov sira/šunke

two steaks
dva zrezka

a half kilogram of strawberries/tomatoes
pol kile jagod/paradižnika

Would you please…?
Ali lahko, prosim…?

cut it into slices
narežete

deliver it
dostavite na dom

add some more
dodate še malo

Communications

Post Office – Phone Communication – Internet –
Emergency Communications – Signs

airmail	**letalska pošta**
cell, mobile phone	**mobilni telefon, mobitel**
e-mail	**elektronska pošta**
fax	**faks**
post office	**pošta**
stamps	**znamke**
telephone	**telefon**

Post Office
(Pošta)

Where is the post office/a mailbox?
Kje je pošta/nabiralnik?

Where can I send a telegram/fax/parcel?
Kje lahko pošljem telegram/faks/paket?

I would like to send this by express mail/airmail.
Želim poslati pismo po hitri pošti/letalski pošti.

When will it arrive in Sydney?
Kdaj bo prispelo v Sydney?

How much does it cost?
Koliko stane?

Please give me an envelope and stamps for a letter
to the US.
Eno kuverto in znamke za ZDA.

I need to send a fax to
   this number.

1 page/6 pages.

**Poslati moram faks na
to številko.**

Ena stran/šest strani.

Would you please give me the confirmation of the
   sent mail?

**Mi lahko, prosim, date potrdilo o oddani
   pošiljki?**

Phone Communication
(Telefonska komunikacija)

cell phone, mobile phone	**mobilni telefon**
dial tone	**klicni ton**
home phone	**telefon doma**
information	**informacije**
network	**omrežje**
office phone	**telefon v službi**
telephone directory	**telefonski imenik**
telephone number	**telefonska številka**
yellow pages	**rumene strani**

Where is a telephone/public phone?
Kje je telefon/telefonska govorilnica?

May I speak to Mr. Kovač, please?
Lahko govorim z gospodom Kovačem, prosim?

This is John Wilson speaking.
John Wilson pri telefonu.

Mr. Kovač isn't in at the moment.
Gospoda Kovača trenutno ni tukaj.

Mr. Kovač is speaking on the other line.
Gospod Kovač govori na drugi liniji.

Would you like to leave a message?
Želite pustiti sporočilo?

May I have the area code for Celje, please?
**Ali mi lahko, prosim, poveste vhodno klicno
  številko za Celje?**

A collect call to Glasgow, please.
Klic na povratne stroške v Glasgow, prosim.

The line is busy.
Linija je zasedena.

Nobody is answering the phone.
Nihče ne odgovori.

All the lines are busy.
Vse linije so zasedene.

Try again later.
Poskusite pozneje.

Call back in half an hour.
Pokličite čez pol ure.

I will call you later.
Te pokličem kasneje.

Call me back.
Pokliči me nazaj.

Please pick up the phone.
Dvigni telefon.

My battery is low (it might disconnect).
Zmanjkuje mi baterij (lahko, da bo prekinilo).

I want to complain about my phone bill.
**Rad(a) bi se pritožil(a) v zvezi z mojim
telefonskim računom.**

May I use your phone?
Lahko pokličem s tvojega/vašega telefona?

I can't hear you well.
Ne sliši se dobro.

The number you are calling is not available. Please
try again later.
**Številka trenutno ni dosegljiva. Prosim,
pokličite pozneje.**

This number doesn't exist.
Ta številka ne obstaja.

Internet
(Internet)

@	**"afna"**
dot-com	**"pika kom"**
e-mail	**elektronska pošta**
homepage	**domača stran**
Internet access	**dostop do interneta**
link	**povezava**
user	**uporabnik**
Web page	**spletna stran**

Where is a cybercafé?
Kje lahko uporabljam Internet?

Where can I find an Internet connection?
Kje se lahko priključim na Internet?

How much is it per hour?
Koliko stane ena ura?

May I check my e-mail?
Lahko pogledam mojo (elektronsko) pošto?

I need to send an e-mail.
Poslati moram (elektronsko) pošto.

This computer doesn't work/is too slow.
Ta računalnik ne dela/je prepočasen.

Emergency Communications
(Urgentna komunikacija)

Help!   Help me!
Na pomoč!   **Pomagajte mi!**

What happened?
Kaj se je zgodilo?

Call the police/fire department/ambulance!
Pokličite policijo/gasilce/zdravniška pomoč!

Please, hurry up!
Pohitite, prosim!

Please, come as soon as possible!
Prosim, pridite čim hitreje!

Signs
(Javna sporočila)

Reserved
Rezervirano

Restroom
Stranišče, WC

Men/Ladies
Moški/Ženske

Today's special
Danes priporočamo

Caution! Roadwork
Pozor! Delo na cesti

No entry
Vstop prepovedan

No smoking
Kaditi prepovedano

No parking
Parkiranje prepovedano

Open/closed
Odprto/zaprto

Money

At the Exchange Office –
At the Bank – Paying Bills

The Slovene currency unit is called a ***tolar*** and consists of one hundred ***stotin***. Currency and coins are decorated with motifs that commemorate the nation's history and countryside.

Please note that the word "***tolar***" varies quite a bit due to the different declensions. Since it's almost impossible to buy something for one tolar, you'll find it useful to remember the plural form, ***tolarjev***.

one tolar
en tolar

two tolars
dva tolarja

three/four tolars
trije/štirje tolarji

five/six tolars
pet/šest tolarjev

one hundred twenty-five tolars
stopetindvajset tolarjev

five hundred tolars
petsto tolarjev

one thousand tolars
tisoč tolarjev

three thousand, five hundred tolars
tri tisoč petsto tolarjev

four hundred thousand tolars
štiristo tisoč tolarjev

half a million tolars
pol miljona tolarjev

At the Exchange Office
(V menjalnici)

amount	**vsota, znesek**
banknote	**bankovec**
change	**drobiž**
coin	**kovanec**
money	**denar**

I would like to change American dollars into
 tolars.
**Rad(a) bi zamenjal(a) ameriške dolarje v
 tolarje.**

What is the exchange rate for the dollar today?
Kakšen je današnji tečaj za dolarje?

I would like to buy 300 euros.
Rad(a) bi kupil(a) tristo evrov.

How much commission do you charge (for this
 amount)?
Koliko znese komisija (za to vsoto)?

Would you, please, give me smaller banknotes/coins/
 a receipt?
**Ali mi lahko date manjše bankovce/kovance/
 potrdilo?**

You may hear...

Your passport, please.
Potni list, prosim.

How many euros would you like to buy?
Koliko evrov želite?

Unfortunately, we are out of Croatian kunas.
Žal nimamo več hrvaških kun.

Canadian dollars must be ordered ahead of time.
Kanadske dolarje morate naročiti vnaprej.

At the Bank
(V banki)

Bank offices in larger cities are accustomed to dealing with foreign customers. You may go to the department called **Poslovanje s tujimi osebami** (International Department) where you will be attended to in English.

bank account	**bančni račun**
bank office	**bančna poslovalnica**
cashier	**blagajna**
checking account	**tekoči račun**
deposit	**polog**
foreign currency division	**poslovanje z devizami**
money transfer	**denarne pošiljke, nakazila**
withdrawal	**dvig**

Where may I cash this traveler's check?
Kje lahko vnovčim ta potovalni ček?

Please sign here.
Prosim, podpišite tukaj.

May I get a cash advance with this credit card?
Ali lahko dvignem gotovino s to kreditno kartico?

I would like to open a bank account.
Rad(a) bi odprl(a) bančni račun.

I'd like to withdraw money from my account.
Rad(a) bi dvignil(a) denar z mojega bančnega računa.

I'd like to open a checking/savings account.
Rad(a) bi odprl(a) tekoči/depozitni račun.

I need your account number.
Potrebujem številko vašega računa.

I would like to send money to Germany.
Rad(a) bi nakazal(a) denar v Nemčijo.

I'd like to close my account in this bank.
Rad(a) bi zaprl(a) moj bančni račun.

I'd like to rent a safe deposit box, please.
Rad(a) bi najel(a) sef.

I would like to pay these bills.
Rad(a) bi plačal(a) te račune.

What time do you close?
Kdaj se banka zapre?

I would like to make a money transfer to the following bank account…
Rad(a) bi nakazal(a) denar na sledeči bančni račun…

I am waiting to receive a money transfer from
 England.
Čakam na prejem denarja iz Anglije.

Anything new?
Je kaj novega?

I will be back in an hour.
Čez eno uro se vrnem.

Paying Bills
(Plačevanje računov)

In bars and restaurants, you normally pay after you
are finished eating or drinking. There are, however,
some bars where you are expected to pay upon
ordering.

change	**drobiž**
credit card	**kreditna kartica**
receipt	**račun**
tip	**napitnina**

How much is it?
Koliko je?

That's 2,500 tolars.
Dva tisoč petsto tolarjev.

Do you accept credit cards?
Sprejmete kreditne kartice?

No, cash only.
Ne, samo gotovino.

May I have a receipt?
Lahko dobim račun?

May we pay separately?
Lahko plačamo posebej?

Keep the change.
Obdržite drobiž.

Shopping & Services

Clothing – Footwear – At the Bookstore –
At the Flower Shop – At the Photo Shop –
At the Barber's/Hairdresser's – At the Laundromat

antique store	**starinarnica**
bookstore	**knjigarna**
department store	**veleblagovnica**
drugstore	**drogerija**
flower shop	**cvetličarna**
food store	**trgovina z živili**
jewelry store	**zlatarna**
market	**tržnica**
pharmacy	**lekarna**
shoe store	**trgovina z obutvijo**
supermarket	**supermarket**
toy store	**trgovina z igračami**

Is there a supermarket/shopping center near here,
   please?
**Je v bližini kakšna trgovina/nakupovalno
   središče?**

What do you want?
Kaj želite?

I'm just looking.
Samo gledam.

Do you have anything made in Slovenia?
Imate kaj slovenskega?

I would like this/that.
Rad(a) bi to/tisto.

May I have some (more) of this, please?
Lahko dobim (še) nekaj tega, prosim?

May I try it on?
Lahko probam/poskusim?

How much does it cost?
Koliko stane?

Would you please discount the price?
Ni nobenega popusta?

When do you expect to get a new shipment?
Kdaj pričakujete novo pošiljko?

When does the sale start?
Kdaj se pričnejo razprodaje?

Where's the cashier, please?
Kje je blagajna?

Do you accept credit cards?
Vzamete kreditne kartice?

May I have a receipt?
Lahko dobim račun?

Would you please wrap this up?
Ali lahko, prosim, zavijete?

Where's the customer service desk?
Kje je oddelek za pritožbe?

Excuse me, I would like to exchange this book/jacket.
Oprostite, želim zamenjati to knjigo/jakno.

It's defective/damaged.
Ima napako.

Do you offer home delivery?
Ali dostavljate tudi na dom?

Do you have a business card/Web site?
Imate poslovno vizitko/spletno stran?

Please, mark on the invoice that I would like my
tax refunded.
Prosim, označite na računu, da želim povrnitev davka.

Clothing
(Oblačila)

Where's the children/men/women's department?
Kje je otroški/moški/ženski oddelek?

What size are you?
Katero številko nosite?

How much is that dress?
Koliko stane ta obleka?

Do you have any larger/smaller shirts?
Nimate nobenih večjih/manjših srajc?

Show me other colors, please.
Mi pokažete, prosim, še druge barve.

Please show me that shirt/those pants.
Mi lahko pokažete to srajco/tiste hlače?

The fitting rooms are on the end.
Kabine za preoblačenje so na koncu.

I would like to return this bag.
Rad(a) bi vrnil(a) to torbo.

small	**majhen**
medium	**srednji**
large	**velik**
longer	**krajši**
shorter	**daljši**
belt	**pas**
blouse	**bluza**
bra	**nedrček**
cardigan	**jopica**
coat	**plašč**
dress	**obleka**
gloves	**rokavice**
handbag	**torbica**
hat	**klobuk**
jacket	**jakna**
pajamas	**pidžama**
panties	**spodnje hlače**
pants	**hlače**
raincoat	**dežni plašč**
scarf	**šal**
shirt	**majica**
skirt	**krilo**
socks	**nogavice**
stockings	**hlačne nogavice**
suit	**suknjič**
sweater	**pulover**
swimsuit	**kopalke**
umbrella	**dežnik**

Footwear
(Obutev)

What size shoes do you wear?
Katera je vaša številka čevljev?

boots	**škornji**
sandals	**sandali**
shoes	**čevlji**
shoe brush	**krtača za čevlje**
shoe polish	**loščilo za čevlje**
slippers	**copati**
tennis shoes	**superge, teniske**
winter boots	**zimski škornji**

At the Bookstore
(V knjigarni)

book	**knjiga**
bookstore	**knjigarna**
dictionary	**slovar**
magazine	**revija**
newspaper	**časopis**
notebook	**zvezek**
poetry	**poezija**
prose	**proza**
science fiction	**znanstvena fantastika**

Do you have a city/road map?
Imate zemljevid mesta/cestni zenljevid?

Do you sell foreign newspapers?
Prodajate tuje časopise?

Do you have newspapers in English/French/German?
Imate časopis v angleščini/francoščini/nemščini?

At the Flower Shop
(**V cvetličarni**)

I would like roses/orchids/carnation.
Hočem vrtnice/orhideje/nagelj.

Please give me seven.
Dajte mi jih sedem, prosim.

How much is this bouquet?
Koliko stane ta šopek?

At the Photo Shop
(**V foto ateljeju**)

I need film/a battery.
Potrebujem film/baterije.

How much for developing the film?
Koliko stane razvijanje filma?

When will it be ready?
Kdaj bodo gotove?

Do you want them to be ready in an hour?
Jih potrebujete čez eno uro?

At the Barber's/Hairdresser's
(**Pri brivcu/frizerju**)

barber	**brivec**
hair	**lasje**
haircut	**pričeska**
hairdresser	**frizer**

A haircut, please.
Striženje, prosim.

Please, cut it just a little.
Prosim, skrajšajte čisto malo.

I would like a shave.
Britje, prosim.

Dye my hair, please.
Želim barvanje, prosim.

Trim my beard/mustache, please.
Pristrižite brado/brke, prosim.

Permanent./Blow dry.
Trajno./Vodno.

Do you like it this way?
Vam je všeč tako?

Yes, it's very nice this way.
Da, zelo mi je všeč.

At the Laundromat
(V pralnici)

dry cleaning	**čistilnica**
laundry	**pralnica**

This is for cleaning/ironing/washing.
To je za čiščenje/likanje/pranje.

When will it be ready?
Kdaj bo gotovo?

Would you repair this, please?
Ali lahko popravite?

Do not wash this in hot water.
Ne perite v vroči vodi.

Sightseeing & Entertainment

Guided Tours – Nightlife – Museums –
TV, Movies & Theater

Where is the tourist information office, please?
Kje se nahajajo turistične informacije?

May I have a town map?
Lahko dobim zemljevid mesta?

What is the name of this market/church/palace?
Kako se imenuje ta trg/cerkev/palača?

Can you tell me where the main monuments are
  located, please?
**Mi lahko, prosim, poveste, kjer se nahajajo
  glavne znamenitosti?**

Is there a picnic area here?
Je tukaj v bližini kakšen prostor za piknike?

Where's the souvenir shop?
Kje je trgovina s spominki?

How old is this castle?
Koliko je star ta grad?

How far is the palace?
Kako daleč je do palače?

May I take photos in here?
Je fotografiranje dovoljeno?

Is entering free?
Je potrebno plačati vstopnino?

Do you accept euros here?
Vzamete evre?

Do you have a group fare?
Imate skupinske vstopnice?

Is there a student discount on tickets?
Kaj pa študentski popust?

May I see your student ID, please?
Lahko vidim vašo študentsko izkaznico, prosim?

Guided Tours
(Vodeni izleti)

I would like to see the city and surrounding areas.
Rad(a) bi si ogledal(a) mesto in njegovo okolico.

We need an English-speaking guide.
Potrebujemo angleško govorečega vodiča.

What kind of excursions do you organize?
Kakšne izlete organizirate?

We would like to go to the museum/to the mountains.
Radi bi šli v muzej/v gore.

Is there a sightseeing bus?
Obstaja ogled znamenitosti iz avtobusa?

Can you tell me when we'll return?
Mi lahko poveste čas povratka?

Nightlife
(Nočno življenje)

bar, nightclub	**bar, nočni klub**
casino	**casino**
dance club	**diskoteka**

Is there a dance club around here?
Je v bližini kakšna diskoteka?

Is entering free?
Je potrebno plačati vstopnino?

Do you know a good nightclub?
Ali poznate kakšen dober nočni klub?

Is there dance music/billiards/a live show?
Imajo plesno glasbo/biljard/live show (show v živo)?

Would you recommend a good nightclub?
Lahko priporočite kakšen dober nočni klub?

How do we get there?
Kako se pride do tja?

Museums
(Muzej)

exposition	**razstava**
gallery	**galerija**
museum	**muzej**

I would like to visit the museum of modern art/ the museum of history.
Rad(a) bi obiskal(a) muzej moderne umetnosti/ zgodovine.

How much is the admission fee?
Koliko stane vstopnina?

Is it open seven days a week?
Je odprt vse dni v tednu?

What time does the museum close?
Kdaj se zapre muzej?

Where can I buy a guidebook to the museum/
exposition?
Kje lahko kupim knjižico o muzeju/razstavi?

TV, Movies & Theater
(Televizija, Kino in Gledališče)

ballet	**balet**
cartoon	**risanka**
cinema	**kino**
coat room	**garderoba**
concert	**koncert**
documentary	**dokumetarni film**
movie	**film**
opera	**opera**
orchestra	**orkester**
performance	**nastop**
play	**igra**
program	**program, (tv) spored**
theater	**gledališče**
TV	**televizija**

Do you have tickets for Nabucco?
Imate vstopnice za predstavo Nabucco?

All tickets are sold out.
Vse vstopnice so razprodane.

Two seats, please.
Dve vstopnici, prosim.

In the front or in the back row?
V sprednjem ali zadnjem delu?

In the center row.
V sredini.

I would like to book four tickets for tonight's
10 o'clock show.
**Rad(a) bi rezerviral(a) štiri vstopnice za
predstavo ob desetih zvečer.**

The show is cancelled/rescheduled.
Predstava je odpovedana/prestavljena.

Aren't the cinema tickets cheaper on Mondays?
Ali niso filmske karte cenejše ob ponedeljkih?

When does the show start?
Kdaj se začne predstava?

May I have a concert program, please?
Lahko dobim program koncerta, prosim?

What time does the next performance start?
Kdaj se prične naslednja predstava?

Where can I get a program?
Kje lahko dobim program?

Who is the writer/the director/the actor?
Kdo je avtor/režiser/igralec?

Where could I watch foreign TV channels?
Kje lahko gledam tuje televizijske postaje?

Health & Hygiene

At the Doctor – At the Dentist –
At the Pharmacy – At the Drugstore

Body
(Telo)

ankle	**gleženj**
arm	**roka**
armpit	**pazduha**
bone	**kost**
brain	**možgani**
chest	**prsa**
elbow	**komolec**
finger	**prst**
foot	**noga**
hand	**roka**
heart	**srce**
heel	**peta**
hip	**bok**
knee	**koleno**
leg	**noga**
muscle	**mišica**
nail	**noht**
neck	**vrat**
nerve	**živec**
rib	**rebro**
shoulder	**rama**
skin	**koža**
spine	**hrbtenica**
stomach	**trebuh**
thumb	**palec**
vein	**vena**
wrist	**zapestje**

Head
(Glava)

ears	**ušesa**
eyes	**oči**
hair	**lasje**
mouth	**usta**
teeth (tooth)	**zobje (zob)**

Organs
(Notranji organi)

blood	**kri**
brain	**možgani**
heart	**srce**
kidney	**ledvica**
liver	**jetra**
lungs	**pljuča**

At the Doctor
(Pri zdravniku)

backache	**bolečine v hrbtenici**
chest pain	**bolečine v prsnem košu**
cold	**prehlad**
diarrhea	**driska**
headache	**glavobol**
pain	**bolečina**
stomachache	**bolečine v trebuhu**

I feel bad.
Slabo se počutim.

He feels bad./She has a serious injury.
On se slabo počuti./Težko je poškodovana.

Excuse me, I need to see a pediatrician.
Oprostite, potrebujem zdravnika pediatra.

Please, call a doctor/an ambulance!
Prosim, pokličite zdravnika/rešilno vozilo!

Please, take me to a hospital!
Prosim, odpeljite me v bolnico!

What is wrong with me?
Kaj mi je?

I have a headache/fever/sore throat.
Imam glavobol/vročino/boleče grlo.

You may hear...

What's the matter?
Kaj je narobe?

Does it hurt?
Boli?

Yes, a little./No.
Da, malo./Ne.

Since when?
Koliko časa?

Lie/sit down.
Uležite/usedite se.

Breathe deeply.
Dihajte globoko.

Please undress to the waist.
Slecite se do pasu.

You have a cold/an inflammation/a fracture.
Imate prehlad/vnetje/zlom.

Take this medicine/these drops/these pills three
times a day.
**Vzamite to zdravilo/te kapljice/te tablete trikrat
na dan.**

At the Dentist
(**Pri zobozdravniku**)

dentist	**zobozdravnik**
filling	**plomba**
gum	**dlesen**
tooth	**zob**
toothache	**zobobol**

I have a toothache.
Boli me zob.

Open your mouth, please.
Odprite usta, prosim.

We'll give you a local anesthetic.
Dali vam bomo lokalno anestezijo.

Eat nothing for next two hours.
Naslednji dve uri ne smete jesti.

At the Pharmacy
(V lekarni)

with prescription	**z receptom**
without prescription	**brez recepta**

Please, give me	**Potrebujem nekaj**
something for…	** proti…**

fever	**vročini**
headache	**glavobolu**
muscle pain	**bolečinam v mišicah**
toothache	**zobobolu**

Do you have…?	**Imate…?**

antibiotics	**antibiotik**
antiseptic	**antiseptik**
aspirin	**aspirin**
bandages	**obvezo**
Band-Aids	**obliž**
eye drops	**kapljice za oči**
thermometer	**termometer**
Vaseline	**vazelin**
vitamins	**vitaminske tablete**

Where is the local veterinarian?
Kje se nahaja najbližji veterinar?

At the Drugstore
(V drogeriji)

Personal accessories and hygeine products can be found in pharmacies, gas stations and drugstores.

body lotion	**mleko za telo**
brush	**krtača**
comb	**glavnik**
conditioner	**balzam**
diapers	**plenice**
eyeliner	**svinčnik za oči**
face cream	**obrazna krema**
hairbrush	**krtača**
hand cream	**krema za roke**
hand towels	**papirnate brisače**
lipstick	**šminka**
mouth rinse	**ustna vodica**
paper tissues	**papirnati robčki**
powder	**puder**
razor	**britev**
shampoo	**šampon**
shaving foam	**krema za britje**
shower gel	**milo za tuširanje**
soap	**milo**
sunscreen	**krema za sončenje**
tampons	**tamponi**
toilet paper	**straniščni papir**
toothbrush	**zobna ščetka**
toothpaste	**zobna pasta**

Doing Business in Slovenia

Business Terms – Written Correspondence

Hello. I am Michael Smith from the Smith
  Clothing Company.
**Pozdravljeni. Jaz sem Michael Smith iz
  tekstilnega podjetja Smith.**

I am here to attend...	**Tukaj sem zaradi...**
a conference	**konference**
an international	**mednarodnega**
committee	**kongresa**
the fair	**sejma**

May I speak with/see Mr. Potočnik?
Bi lahko dobil(a)/videl(a) gospoda Potočnika?

I would like to leave him a message.
Rad(a) bi mu pustil sporočilo.

I would like to set up an appointment.
Rad(a) bi se dogovoril(a) za sestanek.

What time is good for you?
Kdaj vam ustreza?

Where can we meet?
Kje se lahko dobiva?

Come to our office.
Pridite v našo pisarno.

Do you know where Hotel Union is?
Veste kje je hotel Union?

I need an interpreter.
Potrebujem tolmača.

I would like to cancel an appointment.
Rad(a) bi odpovedal(a) sestanek.

business...	**poslovn-i...**
event	**dogodek**
partner	**partner**
visit	**obisk**

business...	**poslovn-o...**
lunch	**kosilo**
relationship	**razmerje**

Business Terms
(Poslovni izrazi)

catalog	**katalog**
contract	**pogodba**
delivery time	**čas dobave**
discount	**popust**
economy	**ekonomija, gospodarstvo**
export/import	**izvoz/uvoz**
fee	**taksa, pristojbina**
foreign investment	**tuja vlaganja**
goods	**blago**
industry	**industrija**
insurance	**zavarovanje**
invoice	**račun, faktura**

offer	**ponudba**
payment	**plačilo**
percent	**odstotek, procent**
price	**cena**
product	**izdelek, proizvod**
production	**proizvodnja**
quality	**kvaliteta**
quantity	**količina**
tax	**davek**
technology	**tehnologija**
trade	**mednarodna trgovina**
VAT	**DDV**
warranty	**garancija**

If you read economic forecasts or statistics, you may find the following terms useful:

average annual growth	**letna povprečna rast**
average gross/	**povprečen bruto/**
net income	**neto dohodek**
following/past year	**prihodnje/preteklo leto**
GDP	**BDP**

Company Departments
(**Oddelki v podjetju**)

administration	**uprava**
distribution	**distribucija**
export	**izvoz**
finance	**finančna služba**
headquarters	**izvršni svet**
import	**uvoz**
legal	**pravna služba**
marketing	**marketing**
personnel	**kadrovska služba**

production	**proizvodnja**
purchase	**nabava**
sales	**prodaja**

Professions
(Poklici)

administrator	**upravnik, upravnica**
advertising agent	**oglaševalec, oglaševalka**
baker	**pek**
chauffeur	**voznik, voznica**
doctor	**zdravnik, zdravnica**
economist	**ekonomist, ekonomistka**
flight attendant	**stevard, stevardesa**
hairdresser	**frizer, frizerka**
interpreter	**tolmač, tolmačka**
journalist	**novinar, novinarka**
judge	**sodnik, sodnica**
lawyer	**odvetnik, odvetnica**
musician	**glasbenik, glasbenica**
painter	**slikar, slikarka**
(computer) programmer	**(računalniški(a))**
	programer,
	programerka
secretary	**tajnik, tajnica**
soldier	**vojak, vojakinja**
teacher	**učitelj, učiteljica**
translator	**prevajalec, prevajalka**
tour guide	**turistični vodič, vodička**
waiter	**natakar, natakarica**

Company Positions
(Delovna mesta)

assistant	**pomočnik, pomočnica**
chairman, chairwoman	**upravitelj, upraviteljica**
department head	**vodja oddelka**
director	**direktor; šef, šefica**
manager	**manager, managerka**
sales agent	**prodajni zastopnik, zastopnica**
sales clerk	**prodajalec, prodajalka**
secretary	**tajnik, tajnica**

Industries
(Sektorji)

agricultural	**kmetijska**
automotive	**avtomobilska**
chemical	**kemijska**
electric	**električna**
entertainment	**zabavna**
film	**filmska**
food and beverage	**prehrambena**
hotel	**hotelska**
metal	**kovinska**
publishing	**založniška**
technology	**tehnološka**
textile	**tekstilna**
wine	**vinska**
wood and furniture	**lesna in pohištvena**

Public Institutions
(Javne Ustanove)

Chamber of Commerce	**Gospodarska zbornica**
Customs Bureau	**carinski urad**
County Court	**okrajno sodišče**
EU Commission	**Komisija Evropske unije**
Parliament	**parlament, skupščina**
Police Station	**policijska postaja**
Supreme Court	**vrhovno sodišče**

Ministry of...	**Ministrstvo za...**

Culture	**kulturo**
Defense	**obrambo**
the Economy	**gospodarstvo**
Education	**šolstvo**
Foreign Affairs	**zunanje zadeve**
Health	**zdravje**
the Interior	**notranje zadeve**
Justice	**sodstvo**

Written Correspondence
(Pisno komuniciranje)

Dear Mr./Mrs./Ms. Novak,
Spoštovani g./Spoštovana ga./gdč. Novak,

I am a representative of the Smith Clothing Company.
Sem zastopnik tekstilnega podjetja Smith.

I was given your address at the Slovene Chamber
   of Commerce.
**Vaš naslov sem dobil(a) na Gospodarski
   zbornici Slovenije.**

I would like to receive your catalogue/business offer.
Rad(a) bi prejel(a) katalog/ponudbo vašega podjetja.

I am interested in the products you display on your Web site.
Zanimajo me izdelki, ki sem jih videl(a) na vaši spletni strani.

I would like to arrange a business appointment.
Rad(a) bi se dogovoril(a) za poslovni sestanek.

Kind regards, (signature)
Lepo pozdravljeni, (podpis)

Sports

Sport Disciplines – Camping – Skiing

When it comes to sports and outdoor activities, Slovenia truly is a paradise. People from all places come to climb the sunny Alps or try whitewater rafting in the beautiful Soča River. Slovenes are enthusiastic sport fans.

champion	**prvak**
championship	**prvenstvo**
coach	**trener**
competition	**tekmovanje**
defeat	**poraz**
favorite	**favorit, najljubši-a**
goal	**gol**
league	**liga**
match	**igra**
medal	**medalja**
net	**mreža**
Olympic Games	**olimpijske igre**
Olympic Torch	**olimpijska bakla**
player	**igralec**
points	**točke**
(to) practice sports	**ukvarjati se z športom**
results	**rezultati**
score	**zadetek**
semi-finals	**polfinale**
spectator	**gledalec**
stadium	**stadion**
team	**ekipa**
track (athletic)	**(atletska) steza**
training	**priprave, trening**
victory	**zmaga**
World Cup	**svetovni pokal**

What is your favorite sport?
Kateri je vaš/tvoj najljubši šport?

I play tennis/chess/cards/football.
Igram tenis/šah/karte/nogomet.

What team do you support?
Za katero ekipo naviješ?

Who won the game?
Kdo je zmagal?

Sport Disciplines
(Športne discipline)

archery	**lokostrelstvo**
athletics	**atletika**
auto racing	**avtomobilske dirke**
badminton	**badminton**
ballooning	**balonarstvo**
baseball	**baseball**
basketball	**košarka**
biathlon	**biatlon**
boat racing	**tekmovanje s čolni, regata**
bodybuilding	**bodibilding**
bowling	**kegljanje**
boxing	**boks**
bungee jumping	**skok z bungeejem**
canoe/kayak	**kanu/kajak**
cards	**karte**
caving	**jamarstvo**
chess	**šah**
cricket	**kriket**
cycling	**kolesarstvo**
diving	**potapljaštvo**

fishing	ribolov
football (American)	**Ameriški nogomet**
football (soccer)	**nogomet**
golf	**golf**
gymnastics	**gimnastika**
hockey	**hokej na ledu**
horseback riding	**jahanje**
hunting	**lov**
ice-skating	**drsanje na ledu**
jogging	**tek, trim**
judo	**judo, džudo**
motocross	**motokros**
motor racing	**motorne dirke**
mountain climbing	**gorsko plezanje**
polo	**polo**
rugby	**ragbi**
running	**tek**
sailing, yachting	**jadranje**
skiing (alpine)	**smučanje (alpsko)**
ski jumps	**smučarski skoki**
slalom	**slalom**
snowboarding	**deskanje na snegu**
speed skating	**hitrostno drsanje**
surf	**surfanje**
swimming	**plavanje**
table tennis, ping pong	**namizni tenis, ping pong**
tae kwan do	**te kvan do**
tennis	**tenis**
triathlon	**triatlon**
volleyball	**odbojka**
water polo	**waterpolo**
weightlifting	**dvigovanje uteži**

Camping
(**Kampiranje**)

Camping is easy to find in all parts of the country. Most campgrounds tend to be close to rivers and forest areas.

tent	**šotor**
camping site	**kamp**

How much does it cost for a two-person tent and a car?
Koliko stane za šotor z dvema osebama in za en avto?

How far are the nearest facilities?
Kako daleč se nahajajo najbližji sanitarni prostori?

Are dogs allowed in this camping site?
Ali je dovoljeno imeti psa?

Skiing
(**Smučanje**)

Skiing is a very popular sport in Slovenia and you can find ski resorts all over the country. The largest Slovene ski resort is Kranjska gora, which is in the country's northwest. Krvavec (less than a 30-minute drive from Ljubljana) is very popular among inhabitants of central Slovenia. People from the Maribor region take a cable car to Pohorje or visit the nearby Rogla. In Kanin, near the Italian border, you can enjoy skiing until spring.

cable car	gondola
chair lift	sedežnica
cross country skis	tekaške smuči
easy/difficult ski slope	lahko/težka smučarska proga
skis	smuči
ski boots	pancerji
ski poles	smučarske palice
ski school	smučarska šola
ski instructor	učitelj smučanja
to ski	smučati
tow rope	vlečnica

One morning/afternoon/day-long ticket, please.
Eno jutranjo/popoldansko/celodnevno karto, prosim.

Where would I find the ski rental?
Kje lahko najdem izposojevalnico smučarske opreme?

I would like to rent ski boots, size 42.
Rad(a) bi si izposodil(a) pancerje številka 42.

Which way are the easy/difficult slopes?
Kje so lažje/težje proge?

Nature

Animals – Plants & Environments –
Weather & Temperature

One-seventh of Slovenia is forestland and many
areas have the status of natural treasures. Slovenians are very proud of their countryside and go to
great lengths to protect it.

bear	**medved**
bee	**čebela**
bird	**ptica**
bull	**bik**
cat	**maček, muc** (*coll.*)
chicken	**kokoš, kura**
cow	**krava**
crocodile	**krokodil**
dog	**pes, kuža** (*coll.*)
duck	**raca**
eagle	**orel**
elephant	**slon**
fish	**riba**
fly	**muha**
fox	**lisica**
frog	**žaba**
goat	**koza**
goose	**gos**
horse	**konj**
lion	**lev**
lizard	**kuščar**
monkey	**opica**
mosquito	**komar**
mouse	**miš, miška** (*coll.*)
octopus	**hobotnica**

salmon	**losos**
shark	**morski pes**
sheep	**ovca**
snail	**polž**
snake	**kača**
tiger	**tiger**
turtle	**želva**
wolf	**volk**
zebra	**zebra**

Plants & Environments
(Vegetacija in Okolje)

The coast of Slovenia is small, but nice. Do not expect to find sandy beaches, but you can enjoy the typical Mediterranean vegetation (pines, oaks, olive trees, bay leaves), cool breezes and pleasant climate. Forests, hills, rivers, and streams are abundant throughout the country. Hiking and trekking are perhaps Slovenian's most popular recreational activities.

bush	**grmovje**
coast	**obala**
desert	**puščava**
flower	**roža, cvetlica**
forest	**gozd**
grass	**trava, zelenica**
hill	**grič, hrib**
leaf	**list**
mountain	**gora**
park	**park**
pasture	**travnik, pašnik**
river	**reka**
sea	**morje**

spring	**izvir**
stream	**potok**
swam	**močvirje**
tree	**drevo**

Weather & Temperature
(Vreme in Temperature)

Winters in Slovenia can be cold and harsh. If you are planning outdoor activities, be sure to check the weather forecast (*vremenska napoved, vremensko poročilo*).

clouds	**oblaki**
eclipse	**lunin mrk**
moon	**luna, mesec**
rain	**dež**
sky	**nebo**
snow	**sneg**
stars	**zvezde**
storm	**nevihta**
sun	**sonce**
weather	**vreme**
wind	**veter**

What is the temperature today?
Koliko stopinj je danes?

What is the weather forecast for today/tomorrow?
Kakšna je vremenska napoved za danes/jutri?

The forecast is…
Napovedovano je…

sunny weather
sončno vreme

cloudy (weather) and rain in the mountain areas
oblačno (vreme) in padavine v gorskih območjih

bad weather with possible snowstorm
slabo vreme z možnimi snežnimi padavinami

hot and dry air in coastal Slovenia
vroč in suh zrak v Primorju

cloudy with partially clear skies
oblačno vreme z delnimi zjasnitvami

good weather conditions with strong wind in the
mountain areas
**ugodne vremenske razmere ter močen veter v
gorskih območjih**

The morning low/day's high temperature will be...
**Najnižje jutranje/najvišje dnevne temperature
bodo...**

The thermometer is at 26 degrees Celsius.
Termometer je pokazal 26 stopnij.

It's raining/snowing.
Dežuje./Sneži.

The temperature has fallen below zero.
Temperature so padle pod nič stopinj.

Will it be a hot/rainy day?
Bo danes vroč/deževen dan?

Do you think it might snow tomorrow?
Mislite, da bo jutri smežilo?

Should I put on my winter clothes?
Naj oblečem zimska oblačila?

Small Talk

Making Friends – Family – Dating

Making Friends
(Med prijatelji)

Are you from around here?
Ali si od tukaj?

What do you do for living?
Kaj si po poklicu?

Can you recommend a good bar/restaurant in the area?
Mi lahko priporočiš kakšen dober bar/kakšno dobro restavracijo v bližini?

Is this a reasonable price?
Je ta cena v redu?

Would you please tell me what the popular hangouts are?
Mi lahko prosim poveš kje se kaj dogaja?

Have you ever been to…?
Ali ste že bili kdaj v…?

This is my first time here.
Prvič sem tukaj.

I enjoy mountain climbing/Slovene food.
Rad(a) imam plezanje/slovensko hrano.

I am having a good time. What about you?
Imam se dobro. Kaj pa ti?

Would you like to go…?
Bi šel (*m.*)/šla (*f.*)…?

Would you help me with the…?
Mi lahko pomagaš pri…?

It was very nice talking to you. See you around.
Lepo se je bilo pogovarjati s tabo. Se vidimo.

Family
(Družina)

aunt	**teta**
cousin	**bratranec** (*m.*), **sestrična** (*f.*)
daughter	**hči, hčerka**
family	**družina**
family tree	**družinsko drevo**
father	**oče, oči** (*coll.*)
grandchild	**vnuk-inja**
grandfather	**dedek**
grandmother	**babica**
mother	**mati, mama, mami** (*coll.*)
relatives	**sorodniki**
son	**sin**
uncle	**stric**

I am married/single/divorced/engaged.
Sem poročen(a)/samski(a)/ločen(a)/zaročen(a).

Do you have any children?
Imate kaj otrok?

I have three children/twins/a baby girl/boy.
Imam tri otroke/dvojčka/punčka/fantek.

I don't have children.
Nimam otrok.

I live alone/with my parents/with my friends.
Živim sam(a)/z starši/s prijatelji.

My wife is pregnant.
Moja žena je noseča.

My grandparents live with us.
Moj dedek in babica živita z nami.

I will introduce you to my family.
Predstavil(a) te bom moji družini.

Dating
(Razmerja)

anniversary	**obletnica**
boyfriend	**fant**
couple	**par**
date	**zmenek, randi** (*coll.*)
friendship	**prijateljstvo**
girlfriend	**punca, dekle**
love	**ljubezen**
relationship	**razmerje**

to like (somebody)
imeti rad (nekoga)

to be seeing (somebody)
hoditi (z nekom)

to fall in love
zaljubiti se

to break up
nehati (*coll.*)

to miss (somebody)
pogrešati (nekoga)

May I sit here/buy you a drink/have your
telephone number?
**Lahko prisedem/povabim na pijačo/dobim
tvojo telefonsko (številko)?**

I find you very amusing/attractive. Could we meet
again?
**Zdiš se mi zelo zabaven(a)/privlačen(a). Se
lahko ponovno vidiva?**

Would you like to go out with me (tomorrow night)?
Bi šla (f.)/šel (m.) (jutri zvečer) z mano ven?

I had a wonderful time.
Imel(a) sem se res lepo.

I will miss you.
Pogrešal(a) te bom.

I like you.
Všeč si mi.

I love you.
Ljubim te.

Maybe we should take a break from each other.
Mogoče bi si morala malce odpočiti en od drugega.

Measurements

Weight – Units – Age – Colors – Materials

Weight
(Teža)

In Slovenia, as in the rest of the Europe, the weight is expressed in grams, kilograms and tons.

one gram of sugar
en gram sladkorja

20 decagrams of butter
dvajset dekagramov masla

I weigh 50 kilos.
Tehtam petdeset kilogramov.

six tons of rice
šest ton riža

Units
(Merske enote)

centiliter	**centiliter**
centimeter	**centimeter**
cubic meter	**kubični meter**
deciliter	**deciliter**
decimeter	**decimeter**
hectoliter	**hektoliter**
kilometer	**kilometer**
liter	**liter**

meter	**meter**
square meter	**kvadratni meter**

In the bars you will often hear people saying "En deci vina, prosim," which is a common expression for a small glass of wine (1 dcl).

Age
(Starost)

How old are you?
Koliko ste stari? *(pl., sing. form.)*
Koliko si star(a)? *(fam.)*

I am 28 years old.
Star(a) sem osemindvajset let.

I am three years older than Polona.
Od Polone sem starejša tri leta.

Matevž is one year younger than me.
Matevž je eno leto mlajši od mene.

When were you born?
Kdaj ste rojeni? *(pl., sing. form.)*
Kdaj si rojen? *(fam.)*

I was born in 1946.
Rojen(a) sem leta tisoč devetsto šestinštirideset.

How old are your children?
Koliko so stari vaši otroci?

They are five and six years old.
Stara sta pet in šest let.

Colors
(Barve)

black	**črna**
blue	**modra**
brown	**rjava**
green	**zelena**
grey	**siva**
ivory	**marfilna**
ochre	**oker**
orange	**oranžna**
purple	**vijolična**
red	**rdeča**
rose	**roza**
white	**bela**
yellow	**rumena**

Materials
(Materiali)

cardboard	**karton**
cardboard box	**kartonasta škatla**
cement	**cement**
cement base	**cementna baza**
ceramic floor	**keramična tla**
ceramics	**keramika**
glass	**steklo**
glass door	**steklena vrata**
granite	**granit**
granite road	**granitna cesta**
metal	**kovina**
metal industry	**kovinska industrija**
plastic	**plastika**
plastic cup	**plastični kozarec**
porcelain	**porcelain**

porcelain cup	**porcelanasta skodelica**
rubber	**guma**
rubber boat	**gumijast čoln**
silk	**svila**
silk shirt	**svilena srajca**
stone	**kamen**
stone house	**kamnita hiša**
terra cotta	**glina**
terra cotta plate	**glinen krožnik**
textile	**blago, tekstil**
textile shop	**tekstilna trgovina**
wood	**les**
wooden house	**lesena hiša**
wool	**volna**
woolen hat	**volnena kapa**

Time

Telling Time – Days of the Week – Months –
Seasons – National Holidays

Telling Time

In Slovenia, the 24-hour clock is used for telling
time with expressions such as *zjutraj* (in the
morning), *dopoldne* (before noon), *popoldne* (in
the afternoon), *zvečer* (in the evening) and *ponoči*
(at night).

At 5 A.M.
Ob petih./Ob petih zjutraj.
The word morning (zjutraj) is occasionally used for
clarity.

At 5 P.M.
Ob petih popoldne./Ob sedemnajstih.
You can say either "at five in the afternoon" or "at
the seventeenth hour."

What time is it?
Koliko je ura?

It is five o'clock.
Ura je pet.

It is half past three.
Ura je pol štirih./Ura je tri in trideset minut.

It is a quarter to six.
**Ura je četrt na šest./Ura je pet in petinštirideset
    minut./Petnajst do šestih.**

When are we leaving?
Kdaj gremo?

Days of the Week
(Dnevi v tednu)

Monday	**ponedeljek**
Tuesday	**torek**
Wednesday	**sreda**
Thursday	**četrtek**
Friday	**petek**
Saturday	**sobota**
Sunday	**nedelja**

Months
(Meseci)

January	**januar**
February	**februar**
March	**marec**
April	**april**
May	**maj**
June	**junij**
July	**julij**
August	**avgust**
September	**september**
October	**oktober**
November	**november**
December	**december**

Seasons
(Letni časi)

winter	**zima**
spring	**pomlad**
summer	**poletje**
fall/autumn	**jesen**

National Holidays
(Državni prazniki)

New Year's Day	**Novo Leto**
Christmas	**Božič**
Easter	**Velika noč**
Mother's Day	**materinski dan**
Father's Day	**očetovski dan**
February 8th	**Prešern's Day**
	(Slovene holiday)
May 1st	**Labor Day**
June 25th	**Independence Day**
summer/winter holidays	**poletne/zimske**
	počitnice

Countries & Nationalities

Countries – Nationalities –
Continents – Languages

Countries
(Države)

Africa	African	African safari
Afrika	**Afričan-ka**	**afriški safari**
America	American	American car
Amerika	**Američan-ka**	**ameriški avto**
Argentina	Argentine	Argentinian friend
Argentina	**Argentinec-ka**	**argentinski prijatelj**
Australia	Australian	Australian crocodile
Australia	**Avstralec-ka**	**avstralski krokodil**
Austria	Austrian	Austrian mountains
Avstrija	**Avstrijec-ka**	**avstrijske gore**
Belgium	Belgium	Belgian waffles
Belgija	**Belgijec-ka**	**belgijski vaflji**
Bosnia	Bosnian	Bosnian river
Bosna	**Bosanec-ka**	**bosanska reka**

Brazil	Brazilian	Brazilian carnival
Brazilija	**Brazilec-ka**	**brazilski karneval**
Bulgaria	Bulgarian	Bulgarian writer
Bolgarija	**Bolgarijec-ka**	**bolgarski pisatelj**
Canada	Canadian	Canadian forest
Kanada	**Kanadčan-ka**	**kanadski gozd**
Chile	Chilean	Chilean folklore
Čile	**Čilenec-ka**	**čilenska folklora**
China	Chinese	Chinese restaurant
Kitajska	**Kitajec-ka**	**kitajska restavracija**
Croatia	Croatian	Croatian coast
Hrvaška	**Hrvat-ica**	**hrvaška obala**
Czech Republic	Czech	Czech castle
Češka	**Čeh-inja**	**češki grad**
Cuba	Cuban	Cuban rum
Kuba	**Kubanec-ka**	**kubanski rum**
Finland	Finnish	Finnish sauna
Finska	**Finec-ka**	**finska savna**

France	French	French bread
Francija	**Francoz-inja**	**francoski kruh**

Germany	German	German company
Nemčija	**Nemec-ka**	**nemško podjetje**

Greece	Greek	Greek olives
Grčija	**Grk-inja**	**grške olive**

Hungary	Hungarian	Hungarian embassy
Madžarska	**Madžar-ka**	**madžarska embasada**

India	Indian	Indian elephant
Indija	**Indijec-ka**	**indijski slon**

Ireland	Irish	Irish beer
Irska	**Irec-ka**	**irsko pivo**

Italy	Italian	Italian pasta
Italija	**Italijan-ka**	**italijanske testenine**

Jordan	Jordanian	Jordanian minister
Jordanija	**Jordanec-ka**	**jordanski minister**

Kenya	Kenyan	Kenyan safari
Kenija	**Kenijec-ka**	**kenijski safari**

Korea	Korean	Korean machine
Koreja	**Korejec-ka**	**korejski stroj**

Macedonia	Macedonian	Macedonian salad
Makedonija	**Makedonec-ka**	**makedonska solata**
Malaysia	Malaysian	Malaysian TV
Malazija	**Malezijec-ka**	**malezijska televizija**
Mexico	Mexican	Mexican group
Mehiko	**Mehičan-ka**	**mehiška skupina**
Montenegro	Montenegrin	Montenegrin tourism
Črna gora	**Črnogorec-ka**	**črnogorski turizem**
Morocco	Moroccan	Moroccan desert
Maroko	**Maročan-ka**	**maroška puščava**
Netherlands	Dutch	Dutch cheese
Nizozemska	**Nizozemec-ka**	**nizozemski sir**
Nigeria	Nigerian	Nigerian culture
Nigerija	**Nigerijec-ka**	**nigerijska kultura**
Poland	Polish	Polish nation
Poljska	**Poljak-inja**	**poljski narod**
Russia	Russian	Russian vodka
Rusija	**Rus-inja**	**ruska vodka**

Saudi Arabia	Saudi Arabian	Saudi Arabian school
Savdska arabija	**Arabec-ka**	**arabska šola**
Serbia	Serbian	Serbian radio
Srbija	**Srb-kinja**	**srbski radijo**
Slovakia	Slovakian	Slovak newpaper
Slovaška	**Slovak-inja**	**slovaški časopis**
South Africa	South African	South African republic
Južna Afrika	**Južnoafričan-ka**	**južnoafriška republika**
Spain	Spanish	Spanish dance
Španija	**Španec-ka**	**španski ples**
Sweden	Swedish	Swedish factory
Švedska	**Šved-inja**	**švedska tovarna**
Switzerland	Swiss	Swiss watch
Švica	**Švicar-ka**	**švicarska ura**
Turkey	Turkish	Turkish bath
Turčija	**Turek-inja**	**turška kopel**
United Kingdom	British	British movie
Velika Britanija, Anglija	**Anglež-inja**	**angleški film**

Yugoslavia	Yugoslavian	Yugoslavian history
Jugoslavija	**Jugoslovan-ka**	**jugoslovanska zgodovina**

Continents
(Kontinenti)

Africa	**Afrika**
Antarctica	**Antarktika**
Asia	**Azija**
Australia	**Avstralija**
Europe	**Evropa**
North America	**Severna Amerika**
South America	**Južna Amerika**

Languages
(Jeziki)

English, Serbian, Croatian, Italian, German, French, and Hungarian (in the northeast) are the most commonly spoken foreign languages in Slovenia.

Arabic	**arabščina**
Chinese	**kitajščina**
Croatian	**hrvaščina**
English	**angleščina**
French	**francoščina**
German	**nemščina**
Hungarian	**madžarščina**
Italian	**italijanščina**
Japanese	**japonščina**
Polish	**poljščina**
Portuguese	**portugalščina**

COUNTRIES & NATIONALITIES

Russian	**ruščina**
Serbian	**srbščina**
Slovene	**slovenščina**
Spanish	**španščina**
Swahili	**svahili**

100% Slovene

The Ljubljana Slang – Slovene Names –
Popular Slovene Proverbs

English	literal Slovene	Ljubljana slang
beer	**pivo**	**pir**
bottle	**steklenica**	**flaša**
cauliflower	**cvetača**	**karfijola**
chewing gum	**žvečilni gumi**	**čigumi**
curious	**radoveden**	**firbčen**
elevator	**dvigalo**	**lift**
haircut	**pričeska**	**frizura**
hairdryer	**sušilec za lase**	**fen**
soap	**milo**	**žajfa**
stairs	**stopnice**	**štenge**
steering wheel	**krmilo**	**volan**
time	**čas**	**cajt**

Slovene Names
(Slovenska imena)

Male names **moška imena**	Female names **ženska imena**
Andrej	Alenka
Anton	Ana
Blaž	Branka
Gašper	Darja
Jaka	Jasna
Janez	Jana
Jernej	Milena

Jure	Katarina
Matej	Marija
Matevž	Maja
Matija	Nataša
Miha	Nina
Peter	Petra
Primož	Polona
Tomaž	Vesna

Popular Slovene Proverbs
(Slovenski pregovori)

He who takes too long to choose gets the scraps!
Kdor dolgo izbira, mu izbirek ostane!

We like guests when they come and also when
   they go.
**Gostov se dvakrat razveselimo: ko pridejo in ko
   odidejo.**

Each man makes his own fortune.
Vsak je sam svoje sreče kovač.

The stupid farmer grows the largest potato.
Neumen kmet ima najdebeljši krompir.

Never look a gift horse in the mouth.
Podarjenemu konju se ne gleda v zobe.

A lie has short legs.
Laž ima kratke noge.

Food is for the stomach, wine is for the soul.
Hrana je za želodec, vino je za dušo.